Britain's Poorest Children

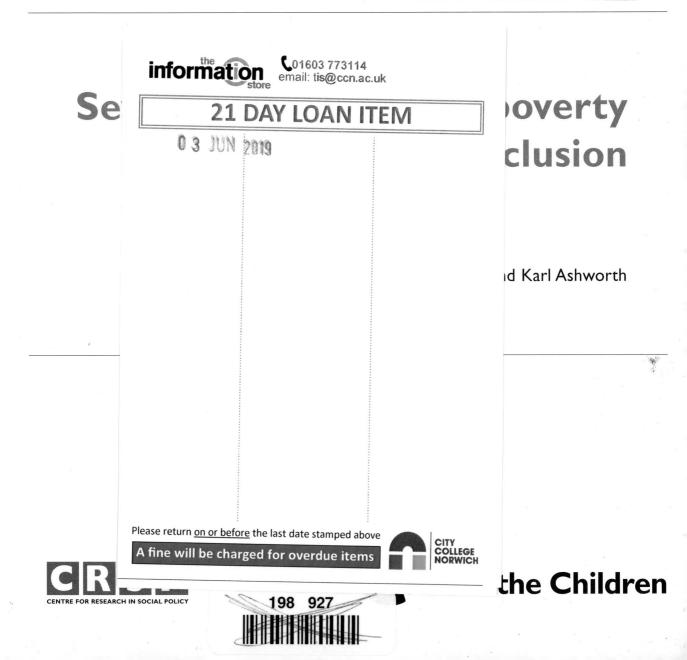

the Children

Save the Children UK is a member of the International Save the Children Alliance, the world's leading independent children's rights organisation, with members in 29 countries and operational programmes in more than 100.

Save the Children works with children and their communities to provide practical assistance and, by influencing policy and public opinion, bring about positive change for children.

Published by
Save the Children
17 Grove Lane
London SE5 8RD
UK

First published 2003

© Save the Children 2003
Registered Charity No. 213890

ISBN 1 84187 081 1

Save the Children gratefully acknowledges the financial contribution for this research from The Lord Mayor's Appeal for Save the Children.

Designed and typeset by Grasshopper Design Company

Contents

Acknowledgements   vii

Executive summary   1
The extent of severe and persistent child poverty   1
Experiences of social exclusion in childhood   2

Part 1 Dimensions of severe child poverty and social exclusion   2
Definition and measurement   2
Which children were in severe poverty?   3
Which children were socially excluded?   3

Part 2 Persistence of severe child poverty   4
Definition and measurement   4
Which children were in persistent and severe poverty?   5
Which children were socially excluded?   6

Part 3 Implications for Britain's poorest children   7

1   Analysis of Britain's poorest children   9
1.1   Defining and measuring persistent and severe child poverty   9
1.2   Defining and measuring social exclusion in childhood   10
1.3   Structure of the report   11
1.4   Data, definition and measurement   12

Part 1 Dimensions of severe child poverty and social exclusion

2   Introduction   15
2.1   How do we, and how should we, measure child poverty?   15
2.2   Measuring social exclusion in childhood   17
2.3   Issues of definition   17

3   Defining severe child poverty   18
3.1   Measures of poverty   18
3.2   Poverty permutations   20
3.3   Defining severe child poverty   21

4   Children experiencing severe poverty   29

4.1   Characteristics of children in severe poverty   29
4.2   Explaining severe poverty   33

5   Poverty and childhood social exclusion   36

5.1   Poverty and social activities exclusion   36
5.2   Poverty and service exclusion   38
5.3   Poverty and exclusion during education   41

6   Poverty and household exclusion   44

6.1   Housing quality   44
6.2   Quality of the local neighbourhood   46
6.3   Financial exclusion   49
6.4   Emotional well-being   51

7   Summary of key findings   53

7.1   Definition and measurement   53
7.2   Which children were in severe poverty?   53
7.3   Which children were socially excluded?   54

Part 2 Persistence of severe child poverty

8   Introduction   57

8.1   Analysing poverty over time   57
8.2   Measuring persistent child poverty   58
8.3   The data   58
8.4   Definition of severe poverty   60

9   Children in persistent and severe poverty   62

9.1   Children in severe poverty   62
9.2   Children in persistent and severe poverty   62
9.3   Transitions between severe, non-severe and no poverty   64
9.4   Summary   67

10 Characteristics of children in persistent and severe poverty 69

10.1 Characteristics of children in persistent and severe poverty 70
10.2 Explaining persistent and severe poverty 87

11 Persistent and severe poverty in childhood and household exclusion 93

11.1 Household financial difficulties 93
11.2 Consumer durables 97
11.3 'Necessities' would like but cannot afford 99
11.4 Problems with accommodation and local area 100

12 Persistent and severe poverty in childhood and exclusion among parents 103

12.1 Parents' satisfaction with local area and home 103
12.2 Parents' civic engagement 105
12.3 Parents' experiences of savings and debt 107
12.4 Parents' emotional well-being 112

13 Persistent and severe poverty in childhood and young people's social exclusion 116

13.1 Young people included in the Youth Questionnaire 116
13.2 Relationships with friends and family 116
13.3 Pocket money and part-time work 121
13.4 School experiences and career aspirations 122
13.5 Emotional well-being 126

14 Summary of key findings 130

14.1 Definition and measurement 130
14.2 Which children were in persistent and severe poverty? 130
14.3 Which children were socially excluded? 131

Part 3 Implications for Britain's poorest children

15 Policy implications   133

15.1	Monitoring policy	133
15.2	The extent and persistence of severe childhood poverty	134
15.3	Benefits	134
15.4	Work	135
15.5	Movements between work and benefits	136
15.6	Lone parents and family transitions	137
15.7	Family size and age of children	137
15.8	Ethnicity	138
15.9	Education	139
15.10	Local area and housing	139
15.11	Geography	140
15.12	Money, savings and debt	140
15.13	Emotional well-being	142
15.14	Children's participation	142
15.15	Measuring child poverty	142

Endnotes   145

References   150

Annexes   153

Annex A	Items and activities regarded as necessary	153
Annex B	Characteristics of children in severe poverty	154
Annex C	Creation of the child and adult deprivation measures	156
Annex D	Significant characteristics explaining non-severe and severe poverty	159
Annex E	Differences between PSE and BHPS net income	160
Annex F	Sample used in Part 2 of this study	161
Annex G	Absolute and equivalised levels of Income Support	163
Annex H	Comparison between children in income and deprivation poverty and those in income only poverty	165
Annex I	Poverty persistence permutations	166
Annex J	Significant characteristics explaining poverty persistence and severity	167
Annex K	Necessity questions in the BHPS and PSE compared	169

Acknowledgements

The authors would like to thank Save the Children UK for the opportunity to investigate such an important topic. In particular, we are grateful to Madeleine Tearse and Katherine Pinnock of Save the Children UK, as well as Cathy Havell, for their support and guidance during the project.

We also greatly appreciate the support of the Joseph Rowntree Foundation which enabled the Poverty and Social Exclusion Survey of Britain (PSE) to be undertaken, and without which Part 1 of this study would not have been possible. Our thanks are also due to colleagues at the Universities of Bristol and York with whom we worked on the PSE, in particular Professor David Gordon and Professor Jonathan Bradshaw. The latter also provided very useful comments on Part 1 of this report.

The UK Data Archive, University of Essex, supplied the British Household Panel Survey (BHPS) Waves 1–9 and the BHPS Derived Current and Annual Net Household Income Variables Waves 1–9 (both deposited by the Institute for Social and Economic Research, University of Essex), for which we are grateful. The Data Archive bears no responsibility for the analysis and interpretation of the data reported here.

Last, but not least, we would like to thank Nicola Selby at the Centre for Research in Social Policy for her excellent administration of the project.

Executive summary

The current Labour government has made a commitment to abolish child poverty in Britain by 2020. In its efforts to do so, a number of targets have been established and indicators of progress are being reviewed annually. However, tackling **severe** child poverty does not feature in these targets or indicators. In fact, although there is now a wealth of information about child poverty in Britain, very little is known about either the extent of severe child poverty or the children who are affected. As a result, we do not know whether different policy measures are required to move these children out of poverty.

To try and fill this knowledge gap, Save the Children UK commissioned the Centre for Research in Social Policy to investigate severe child poverty. Two areas of particular importance were identified: material deprivation combined with low income as an indicator of severe poverty and the extent to which severe poverty persists over time. Therefore, in this study severe child poverty was defined and analysed in two ways:

1 children who experienced a combination of household income poverty, child deprivation and parental deprivation

2 children who lived in households that experienced income poverty which was both persistent and severe.

The research also aimed to establish whether severely poor children were more likely to experience different dimensions of social exclusion than other children. A wide range of dimensions was investigated but, broadly speaking, covered exclusion from:
- social activities
- services (including education) and citizenship
- friendships and support
- living in adequate housing or in an adequate local area
- financial security.

The extent of severe and persistent child poverty

Severe poverty affected a relatively large proportion of children in Britain:
- In 1999, 8 per cent of children experienced a combination of income poverty, child deprivation and parental deprivation.
- Of children analysed over various five-year periods between 1991 and 1999, 9 per cent experienced income poverty that was both persistent and severe.

Children most likely to experience **severe** poverty, using both measures, were those:
- living in a household in receipt of Income Support or Jobseeker's Allowance
- living in a household with no workers
- with a large number of children and/or young children in the household
- living in local authority accommodation
- living in the Midlands (although it should be noted that the numbers of children surveyed in Scotland and Wales were small, so it is difficult to draw conclusions for these countries)

- whose parents had no, or low, educational qualifications
- living in a lone parent family
- of non-white ethnicity.

In addition, **persistent and severe** income poverty was more likely to occur for children in households which experienced one or more changes:
- in their main source of annual income (from benefits to work or vice versa)
- in the number of workers in the household (from no workers to one worker, or vice versa)
- in their family type (from a couple to a lone parent household, in particular).

Experiences of social exclusion in childhood

Social exclusion was measured from three different perspectives:
- exclusion experiences that would affect the whole household
- parents' experiences of exclusion that were also likely to impact on the child
- children's own experiences of social exclusion.

Levels of social exclusion were generally higher amongst children experiencing severe poverty than among other children. Defining severe poverty using a combination of income and deprivation, there were very clear distinctions between severely poor and other children on the majority of measures. Severely poor children were, for example, the most likely to be unable to afford to participate in social activities, to lack access to local services and to live in a poor quality neighbourhood.

Using a persistent and severe income poverty measure, in all cases children experiencing some form of poverty were more likely to experience social exclusion than non-poor children. However, children in persistent income poverty, whether or not their poverty was severe, were the most likely to experience social exclusion themselves, for example they were the least likely to receive pocket money and to undertake part-time work. They were also the most likely to have parents who experienced exclusion, for example their parents were the least likely to be able to make savings, to be engaged in civic activities or to have good mental health.

Part 1 Dimensions of severe child poverty and social exclusion

Definition and measurement
Using the Poverty and Social Exclusion Survey of Britain (PSE), child income poverty and deprivation was measured using a combination of three definitions:
- the child's own deprivation – the child going without one or more 'necessities' because they could not be afforded
- the deprivation of their parents – the parents going without two or more 'necessities' because they could not be afforded
- the income poverty of their household – the household having an income of below 40 per cent of median.

Children were defined as those aged 16 years or less.

The three poverty measures created eight poverty permutations:
- not poor on any measure
- income poor only
- child deprivation only
- parent deprivation only
- income poor and child deprivation
- income poor and parent deprivation
- child and parent deprivation
- poor on all three measures.

Children were defined as being in severe poverty if they were poor on all three measures. This was because children in this group:
- had the lowest average incomes
- were most likely to lack the 'most important' necessities
- lacked the greatest number of necessities – both the children themselves and their parents – and
- had the highest levels of current subjective poverty.

Using this definition, **8 per cent of British children – approximately one million – were severely poor and 37 per cent non-severely poor** (poor on one or two of the three measures).

Which children were in severe poverty?
Both severely poor children and non-severely poor children could be identified by the following characteristics (when all other characteristics were taken into account):
- living in a household with no workers
- living in the South of England
- having parents with no educational qualifications

- living in local authority rented accommodation.

However, severely poor children were more likely to have the first three of these characteristics than non-severely poor children.

In addition, severely poor children were much more likely to have three other characteristics that distinguished them from non-poor children, and which did not identify non-severely poor children. These were:
- living in a household receiving Income Support or Jobseeker's Allowance
- living in the Midlands of England
- being of non-white ethnicity.

Which children were socially excluded?
The PSE includes three areas that might indicate social exclusion in childhood:
- exclusion from social activities
- exclusion from local services
- exclusion during education.

The data also include household and parental measures of social exclusion that are likely to have an impact on children and which parents may find particularly difficult to remedy. These were identified as:
- exclusion through poor housing quality
- exclusion through poor neighbourhood quality
- financial exclusion
- exclusion through poor parental mental well-being.

With a few exceptions, social exclusion was strongly associated with severe poverty. On all of the dimensions studied, there was no apparent difference in the **pattern** of exclusion whether the child was not poor, non-severely poor or severely poor. Rather, in general, the greater the severity of poverty, the greater the number of individual services/activities from which a child was excluded or the greater the number of problems the child experienced. In other words, severe poverty does not lead to a different **form** of exclusion to that experienced by children who are not poor or not severely poor; rather it is different in its **degree**. Severely poor children were, quite simply, excluded from a greater number of services/ activities or experienced a greater number of problems than non-severely poor and non-poor children.

For example:

- Severely poor children showed a much higher rate of being unable to afford to participate in children's social activities than their non-severe poor and non-poor counterparts. The average non-participation rate for severely poor children was 25 per cent compared to 7 per cent for non-severely poor children and just 2 per cent for non-poor children.
- Severely poor children were more likely to be excluded from local services – either because they could not be afforded or accessed. Of severely poor children, 11 per cent were excluded, compared with 8 per cent of non-severely poor children and 5 per cent of non-poor children.
- Severely poor children were more likely to experience problems with their local area. Of severely poor children, 35 per cent experienced problems with their local area compared with 21 per cent of non-severely poor children and 11 per cent of non-poor children.

In terms of the quality of their housing, both severely and non-severely poor children were much more likely to experience poor housing quality than non-poor children. Housing problems were experienced by 16 per cent of severely poor children and 14 per cent of non-severely poor children, compared with 6 per cent of non-poor children.

Part 2 Persistence of severe child poverty

Definition and measurement

At present, there is no one data source that measures income, child deprivation and adult deprivation over time, so that the definition of severe child poverty used in Part 1 of the report could not be used to analyse persistent and severe poverty. Therefore, an income definition had to be used for the measurement of persistent poverty. For consistency, severe and non-severe poverty thresholds were created by determining the median income of children experiencing severe and non-severe poverty, as defined by the income poverty and deprivation measure in Part 1. These equated to 27 per cent and 59 per cent of weekly median household income, respectively.

Using the British Household Panel Survey (BHPS) for the years 1991–1999, children were analysed over various five-year periods (from the ages of 0 to 4 years, 5 to 9 years, 10 to 14 years or 15 to 19 years). For each of the five years it was calculated whether children were in severe, non-severe or no poverty.

Persistent poverty was defined as occurring when children experienced poverty (severe or non-severe) in three out of the five years for which they were analysed – this affected 29 per cent of children. Severe poverty was defined as occurring if children experienced severe poverty in at least one of the five years – this affected 13 per cent of children. Using these criteria, five poverty persistence and severity groups were established:

- **no poverty** – not in poverty in any of the five years
- **short-term poverty only** – less than three years in poverty and no years in severe poverty
- **short-term and severe poverty** – less than three years in poverty but at least one year in severe poverty
- **persistent poverty only** – three or more years in poverty but no years in severe poverty
- **persistent and severe poverty** – three or more years in poverty and at least one year in severe poverty.

Nine per cent of British children were estimated to have experienced persistent and severe poverty over the five-year period for which they were studied.

Which children were in persistent and severe poverty?

Children who experienced **any form of poverty** over the five-year period were different in a number of ways from children who never experienced poverty. Children experiencing poverty were all **more** likely (when all other characteristics were held constant) to have:

- been in a no worker household for one year

- lived in rented accommodation for five years
- had adults in the household who were ill for between three and four years
- lived in the Midlands
- lived in households which received benefits for three or four years
- lived in a household with an average of three or more children.

In addition, children in poverty were all **less** likely to have had parents educated to degree level than children never in poverty.

Characteristics that distinguished children who experienced both **persistent and severe poverty** from children in persistent poverty only were that children in persistent and severe poverty were significantly **less** likely to have been in:

- a lone parent family for five years
- a household that never had work as a main source of annual income (measured in the year prior to the interview)
- a household that moved from no to two workers (or vice versa).

They were **more** likely to have been in households that had:

- no workers in all years (measured at the time of interview)
- two or more transitions in their main source of annual income
- an average of three or more children in the household
- parents educated to degree level or A-level.

It appears that there were at least two distinct groups of children in persistent and severe poverty as defined by their work and benefit characteristics:

1 The first group were those whose financial situation appeared relatively stable, although very bleak. This group included children who had lived in workless households for all of the five-year period and who were also most likely to have spent all five years dependent on benefits as a main income source, further increasing their chances of persistent and severe poverty.

2 The second group were those who experienced income volatility, ie, two or more income transitions between work/other income and benefit income as their main source of income. Children whose households underwent two or more such transitions were much more likely to be in persistent and severe poverty than children who did not experience these transitions. As these children experiencing multiple changes in their main source of income must also have spent at least one year in receipt of benefits, it is likely that their actual chances of experiencing persistent and severe poverty were compounded further.

Children in persistent and severe poverty were **less** likely to have spent all of the five-year period in a lone parent family. This is not to say that children in lone parent families were missing from the group in persistent and severe poverty. Rather, that once their other circumstances were taken into account, children in stable lone parents families were less likely to face persistent and severe poverty than children who constantly lived in a couple family.

Which children were socially excluded?

Reflecting the available measures in the BHPS, social exclusion was measured from three different perspectives:
* the exclusion experiences that would affect the whole household
* parents' experiences of exclusion that were also likely to impact on the child
* the young person's own exclusion experiences at the age of 14 years.

In general, on the **household measures of exclusion** all children in poverty, whatever its persistence or severity, fared much worse than children who had not experienced poverty in any of the five years. There was a very slight trend for children in persistent poverty, with or without severity, to be more likely to have been excluded on a minority of measures (namely to have experienced some financial difficulties, to lack commonly owned consumer durables and to lack 'necessities' because they could not be afforded), but, in general, differences between the poverty groups were small.

However, a much clearer divide between the poverty groups was seen on the measures of **parents' experiences of exclusion**. Once again, in general, children in any form of poverty were more likely to have parents who had experienced exclusion than children never in poverty, but children in persistent poverty, with or without severity, were more likely than the other poverty groups to have parents who had done so. The parents of children in persistent poverty, whether or not the poverty was severe, were **less** likely:
* to be satisfied with the neighbourhood in which they lived

- to be engaged in civic activity (for example voting or active membership of organisations)
- to be able to save or to save as much
- to have high levels of emotional well-being.

An analysis of the **social exclusion experiences of children** at the age of 14 (based on their poverty persistence and severity between the ages of 10 and 14) suggested that young people experiencing poverty were no worse off in terms of:
- their relationships and satisfaction with friends
- their experiences at school
- their level of belief that they were a likeable person.

However, they did seem to be affected by life on a low income in other ways. Young people in persistent and severe poverty:
- received the lowest level of pocket money
- along with children in persistent poverty only, were the least likely to have part-time jobs and, when they did so, worked fewer hours and for less money than other children
- appeared more likely to have strained relationships with their parents, being the least likely to talk to their parents about things that mattered or to be happy with their family
- were least likely to be happy with their appearance and, indeed, with their life as a whole.

Young people appear to be very much affected, at least in some aspects of their lives, by their experiences of poverty. This highlights the importance of being concerned with the impact of poverty on children's current lives **as children**,

not just because of the effects poverty may have on children's future experiences as adults (as so much research seems to do).

Part 3 Implications for Britain's poorest children

The findings imply the importance of:
- providing adequate (financial) support when households are not in work and support for transitions into and out of work
- ensuring adequate (financial) support when transitions in family type occur
- ensuring that parents and children obtain adequate educational qualifications
- improving the living conditions of children in poverty in terms of their housing quality and local area
- supporting families in their efforts to save money in good times and to keep debts to a minimum during bad
- ensuring that parents and children have adequate emotional support and well-being to undertake their roles as such
- adequately (financially) supporting families with a large number of children and/or with young children in the household
- increasing the opportunities for children in poverty to access leisure and social activities.

Further investigation is required to understand, in particular:
- the increased levels of deprivation among children and parents of non-white ethnicity
- the increased levels of severe poverty among children in the Midlands.

A number of conclusions were also reached with regard to the measurement of child poverty:

- An important step forward for the analysis of child poverty would be the inclusion of deprivation-based measures of poverty in longitudinal surveys in order to understand the circumstances under which income becomes inadequate to provide necessities and, in turn, when income becomes adequate to do so.
- Including child-based measures of poverty (and social exclusion) is crucial for an understanding of children's circumstances. Including children in the definition and measurement of these wherever possible and appropriate would lead to further advances in our understanding.
- The study emphasises the multiple manifestations of poverty and social exclusion and, therefore, the need to ensure that these are measured **in the same survey** in order to understand these different manifestations and their inter-relationships. As a result, policy would be better informed.

1 Analysis of Britain's poorest children

The Labour government, first elected in 1997, has made a commitment to ending child poverty within 20 years, halving it within 10 years and reducing it by at least a quarter by 2004. In pursuit of these goals a range of policies to tackle child poverty has been introduced.

The government's 'Household's Below Average Income' series reports that child poverty (measured as children with an equivalised[1] household income below 60 per cent of the median) fell from 25 per cent in 1996/97 to 21 per cent in 2001/02 (Department for Work and Pensions, 2003a). However, independent research has suggested that, following the government's reforms, some children, particularly the poorest, will have experienced decreases in income: 'nearly one in six children in the bottom decile – 300,000 children – are worse off as a result of the reforms' (Sutherland, 2001, p.4). This illustrates the difficulties that the government faces in removing the poorest children from poverty; it may be relatively easy to lift large numbers of children above the poverty line, but potentially more difficult to impact on the circumstances of those who are most severely poor.

Yet, despite the vast array of recent research on child poverty, Save the Children UK became aware that very little is known about the circumstances and characteristics of children in the most severe poverty for whom policy responses may need to be different. Therefore, Save the Children UK commissioned the Centre for Research in Social Policy to undertake research that could begin to develop our understanding of the extent of severe child poverty in the UK[2] and identify the children most likely to be affected.

1.1 Defining and measuring persistent and severe child poverty

Currently the UK Government and the European Union usually measures child poverty by counting the number of children in households with incomes below 60 per cent of contemporary median income. At the time of writing, preliminary conclusions to the government's consultation on how child poverty should be measured have just been released (Department for Work and Pensions, 2003b). These conclusions highlight a number of areas of further work that the government is interested in taking forward and include some discussion of measuring the persistence and depth of poverty. However, although the government currently includes a measure of persistent poverty as an indicator of progress in its annual poverty report *Opportunity for All* (see Chapter 8), at the present time no measure of severe poverty is included.

Therefore, the first question for this study was how severe child poverty should be defined and measured. The authors and Save the Children UK felt that there were two main aspects of severe child poverty that were insufficiently understood and which could be usefully investigated with available data: material deprivation combined with low income as an indicator of severe poverty; and the extent to which severe poverty persists over time.

These two aspects are discussed in greater detail in Parts 1 and 2 of this report. However, to summarise: defining severe child poverty using a combination of income poverty and material deprivation is important in order to identify children in households that not only have a lack of current resources (income), but also cannot afford the basic necessities of life in Britain going into the 21st century (deprivation). While such an approach has not been undertaken previously to any great extent in Britain, a similar definition of poverty is used in Ireland's National Anti-Poverty Strategy (see Layte et al., 2000, for details). However, the UK Government appears to have accepted the value of including deprivation measures of poverty in official surveys: 'The Department for Work and Pensions is considering which deprivation indicators could be usefully added to the Family Resources Survey' (Department for Work and Pensions, 2003b, p.43).

The second aspect of the research, the persistence of child poverty in Britain, has been investigated by other researchers using income measures of poverty (see, for example, Hill and Jenkins, 2001; Ermisch et al., 2001). However, such studies have not investigated the persistence of **severe** poverty. It should be noted that longitudinal data for Britain (that is, data that record the changing circumstances of the same children over time) do not (yet) include measures of material deprivation. As a result, analysis of poverty over time can only use an income definition, so that Part 2 of the report, dealing with the persistence of severe poverty, focuses on the persistence of severe **income** poverty. Despite this limitation, the analysis can help to answer important questions,

such as whether children with the lowest incomes are the most likely to remain poor, whether the severity of poverty affects persistence, and whether children who have experienced severe and persistent poverty differ from children who have not experienced severe poverty.

1.2 Defining and measuring social exclusion in childhood

It is well known that poverty is associated with worse life experiences for children along many dimensions, for example in health, housing, education and employment.[3] The government has increasingly recognised this:

> '...our current understanding of poverty... pays particular attention to income, but goes wider to encompass dimensions of work, education, health, housing and environment.'
>
> Department for Work and Pensions, 2002a, p.1

Whether these dimensions can be packaged and labelled 'social exclusion' in childhood is another matter, and one that cannot be debated at length in this report. Social exclusion remains a contested term that is subject to a multiplicity of definitions, which are most often applied to adult experiences.[4] The government's own definition of social exclusion is 'A short-hand term for what can happen when people or areas suffer from a combination of linked problems such as unemployment, poor skills, low incomes, poor housing, high crime environment, bad health and family breakdown' (Social Exclusion Unit, 2001, p.10). But these problems, as Micklewright

(2002, p.3) has pointed out, are 'a description of examples of circumstances that may lead to exclusion', rather than a definition of social exclusion itself.

Nevertheless, measures of what might be seen as 'social exclusion' in childhood are being devised and used by the government, not least in its targets for children in the annual poverty report, *Opportunity for All*. These include improving educational standards, reducing truancy and exclusions from school, improving housing standards and a number of health-related indicators (Department of Social Security, 1999). Improvements have been reported in many of these areas (Department of Social Security, 2000; Department for Work and Pensions, 2001 and 2002a), although the data for these indicators come from different sources so that it is not possible to identify any overlaps between the measures. However, what would seem of obvious importance in policy terms is to explore whether these 'experiences', 'outcomes' or 'exclusions' in childhood affect poor children to a greater extent than children who are not poor. In other words, if the group of children who are in (severe) poverty is completely different from the group of children who experience the different dimensions of 'social exclusion', this would suggest a different set of policy responses than if the two groups contained the same children.

Therefore, an additional aim of this study was to investigate the extent to which (severe) poverty and 'social exclusion' overlapped, using the term 'social exclusion' as a convenient shorthand for some of these negative experiences in childhood.

1.3 Structure of the report

Part 1 of the report begins with a brief description of some of the advantages and disadvantages of using income measures of poverty. It outlines the measure of deprivation in the Poverty and Social Exclusion Survey of Britain, analysis of which forms the basis of this part of the report, and the measures of social exclusion available in this survey (Chapter 2). In Chapter 3, three dimensions of poverty and their possible permutations are examined to see which permutation might best define 'severe child poverty'. Chapter 4 investigates a range of characteristics of children and their families in severe poverty and determines which of these characteristics best explains their presence in the group of severely poor children. Whether or not poverty and social exclusion are experienced by the same children is addressed by considering the overlaps between child poverty and child-based measures of social exclusion in Chapter 5, and between child poverty and household measures of social exclusion in Chapter 6. Chapter 7 provides a summary of the key findings.

Part 2 of the report begins by suggesting why measuring the persistence of poverty is important, describes the data used in this part of the report (the British Household Panel Survey) and outlines how the sample of children for analysis was devised (Chapter 8). The definition of persistent and severe poverty is established in Chapter 9. Chapter 10 examines the characteristics of children in persistent and severe poverty. The experiences of social exclusion among children in persistent and severe poverty are compared to those of other children in Chapters 11–13. Part 2 concludes with a summary of its key findings (Chapter 14).

Part 3 – the final chapter (Chapter 15) – outlines the main policy implications arising from Parts 1 and 2 of the report and seeks to provide some answers to the question, 'Where next for research and policy for severely poor children?'

1.4 Data, definition and measurement

We have tried to make the report as accessible as possible to the lay reader by leaving out as much technical and statistical detail as possible. Readers interested in finding out more about the statistical procedures and definitions used should refer to the endnotes to the report and/or, for Part 1, to a working paper that can be obtained from the authors (Adelman et al., 2003). However, some comments on the data used and on measurement and definition are necessary to allow the report to be understood.

1.4.1 A child focus
An important aspect of this research is the fact that it uses the child rather than the family as the unit of analysis. For example, the analysis describes the proportion of children in poverty, the proportion of children in workless households, the proportion of children experiencing poor housing and so on. The extent to which the research could be child centred was limited, however, by the fact that both surveys had the household as their main focus. As a result the majority of the survey data analysed were collected from adults within the household rather than from children and young people themselves

(the exception is the British Household Panel Survey's Youth Questionnaire, see Chapter 13 for details). For a true child-focused analysis, surveys of children in families, rather than of families with children, in which as much information as possible is collected directly from children and young people, are required.

1.4.2 The datasets
As the previous section highlighted, Parts 1 and 2 of this report are based on different datasets, each of which is described in greater detail in the introductory chapter of the relevant Part of the report.

Different datasets had to be used because the two parts of the report had different aims. The aim of Part 1 was to try and develop a new measure of severe child poverty based on income and deprivation and to determine how severe child poverty defined in this way related to measures of social exclusion. The Poverty and Social Exclusion Survey of Britain contains the only suitable data, in that it included measures of poverty for both adults and children, and specifically attempted to operationalise and measure social exclusion for both adults and children.

Part 2 had the very different aim of investigating the persistence of severe poverty. This required longitudinal data – that is, data that followed the same children over a number of consecutive years. For Britain the only data available of this type are from the British Household Panel Survey. These data also contain measures that might be seen as capturing (some) similar dimensions of 'social exclusion'. These measures have been used in what should be seen as an initial attempt to understand the relationship(s) between the different measures of severe income poverty and 'social exclusion'.

As with all major datasets used for poverty analysis, the samples for the two datasets analysed in this report were of private households in Britain. In other words, persons/households in institutions, who were homeless or who were highly geographically mobile were excluded from the surveys. For children this means that those living in, for example, children's homes, hospices or bed and breakfast accommodation, or whose families move frequently cannot be included in this type of analysis. Therefore, the circumstances of some of the most deprived and excluded children in Britain are not reported here.

1.4.3 Income data

The two parts of the research use average household income in the definition of poverty to different degrees. Again, detailed descriptions of the income data are provided in the relevant sections of the report. However, it is worth emphasising here that in both Part 1 and Part 2 the income data used are before housing costs have been taken into account. The difference between 'before housing costs' and 'after housing costs' measures of income is important when determining poverty status. With a before housing costs measure, the median income poverty line (and the proportions below it) is calculated using a household's income before housing costs have been deducted. In an after housing costs measure, housing costs are deducted from household income before the median income (and proportions below it) are calculated. The choice of income measure can clearly have important consequences for whether or not households are

below or above the poverty line. An after housing costs measure is, arguably, a better measure of the disposable income households have to spend on necessities and it would have been our preferred measure.[5] However, the only income measure available in the Poverty and Social Exclusion Survey of Britain is a before housing costs measure. Therefore, for consistency (and in line with the government's measure of persistent poverty) Part 2 of the report also uses a before housing costs measure. This means that those with high housing costs could be wrongly identified as not being in poverty because their high housing costs, if taken into account, might well have left them with incomes below the poverty line. Conversely, those with no/low housing costs may be wrongly identified as being in poverty. Therefore, if the study was undertaken using after housing costs measures of poverty it is possible that some different findings might emerge, particularly in relation to specific geographical areas. For example, high housing costs in London would be likely to have an impact on the results for children living there.[6]

1.4.4 Sufficient numbers for analysis

When using data it is essential that there are sufficient numbers of children included in each piece of analysis to be sure that the findings are reliable. In deciding how many children are 'sufficient', we have followed the conventions of Eurostat (the European Commission Statistical Office), which state that results of analysis based on fewer than 20 unweighted or 'real' cases (in this report, children) may be unreliable. Therefore, throughout the report findings that are based on fewer than 20 children are marked in the tables by being bracketed. This is not to say that these findings are not accurate, rather that their accuracy cannot be completely relied upon.

1.4.5 Reading the tables

All tables which show percentages are marked as either 'cell per cent', 'row per cent' or 'column per cent'. This informs the reader as to how the table should be read. 'Row per cent' means that each row of the table totals 100 per cent and 'column per cent' means that each column of the table totals 100 per cent. It should be noted that not all rows or columns in these tables total exactly 100 per cent because of the rounding up or down of decimal places. 'Cell per cent' means that neither the column nor the row adds to 100 per cent – the cell value is simply a free-standing result and it has no relation to the other cells in the column/row. An explanatory note on these terms is appended to the first three tables in which they appear (Tables 3.1, 3.3 and 3.5).

Part 1 Dimensions of severe child poverty and social exclusion

2 Introduction

This part of the report has two main aims:

1 to find a new way of measuring severe child poverty that goes beyond one-dimensional income-based definitions of poverty so that the measure can describe, and take into account, the material deprivation experienced by poor children and their parents

2 to examine the relationships between severe child poverty and some possible dimensions of social exclusion in childhood.

This chapter opens with a summary of some of the advantages and disadvantages of income-based measures of poverty. It then describes the data used in this part of the report – the Poverty and Social Exclusion Survey of Britain – its poverty measure and its measures of social exclusion for children. Finally, some issues of definition specific to this part of the report are outlined.

2.1 How do we, and how should we, measure child poverty?

The most common method used to define, measure and analyse (child) poverty in the UK and, indeed, most other countries, is to count the number of children living in households whose incomes fall below a particular proportion of average household income. As noted in the previous chapter, the UK Government and the European Union generally use a cut-off point of '60 per cent of median equivalised household income' to define poverty.

2.1.1 The advantages of income measures
Income measures of poverty have certain desirable features:
- They provide an estimate of the financial resources available to a household.
- They are easy to use.
- They allow relatively simple cross-country comparisons to be made.

In addition, because information on income has been collected consistently over many years, income provides the only measure of changes in childhood poverty over time (see Part 2). For these reasons income is, and will remain, an important measure of child poverty for the foreseeable future.

2.1.2 The disadvantages of income measures
However, income measures have a number of limitations in measuring poverty, particularly in childhood:
- The basis of income measures is not easy to understand. For example, the UK Government's definition of income poverty is '60 per cent of median equivalised household income (before or after housing costs, including or excluding the self-employed)'.

- The poverty line is arbitrary. There is no scientific reasoning for it being placed at 60 per cent of median income, rather than, say, 50 per cent. So, in real terms, there may be little difference between the child just above the poverty line and the child just below the poverty line.
- There is nothing to say what the income poverty line represents in terms of living standards – whether 60 per cent of the median, for example, provides an adequate standard of living.
- Similarly, using a headcount measure of poverty (such as 60 per cent of median) takes no account of the depth of poverty. A child will be considered 'poor' whether he or she is just below the poverty line or very far below the poverty line.
- It assumes that children share the living standards of the family because it is the income of the whole household that is being measured – if the household as a whole is poor then income measures assume that the children in that household must also be poor.
- Equivalence scales used in income poverty measurement underestimate the cost of children to a family. If more accurate measures of the costs of children were used, it is likely that the extent of child poverty would be seen to be greater.
- Income poverty does not tell us what poor children go without that non-poor children do not: how do their lives differ?
- Income poverty cannot tell us anything about 'social exclusion'.

2.1.3 A different approach to measuring poverty

Despite these widely acknowledged problems (including the government's own consultation document *Measuring Child Poverty* (Department for Work and Pensions, 2002b)), income is often the only measure of poverty that is available to researchers. However, in 1999 a new survey was undertaken: the Poverty and Social Exclusion Survey of Britain (PSE) (Gordon et al., 2000). Developed by researchers at the Universities of Bristol, York and Loughborough, and supported by the Joseph Rowntree Foundation, the survey was designed with the specific aim of measuring different dimensions of poverty and social exclusion in the lives of adults and children in Britain going into the 21st century.

One of the most important features of the PSE is the inclusion of indicators of deprivation for adults and children. These indicators can be used to produce separate measures of poverty for adults and children, in each of which poverty is defined as an enforced lack of items and activities that the majority of the population deem to be necessary. In other words, poverty is going without necessary items and activities because they cannot be afforded, not through choice (Townsend, 1979; Mack and Lansley, 1985; Gordon and Pantazis, 1997).

The extent to which adults and children are deprived of these items and activities can be used to create poverty or 'deprivation' measures for adults and children that overcome some of the disadvantages of measuring poverty using income, particularly for children, in that:

- they produce poverty lines specifically related to adults or children, rather than the household as a whole
- the lines are not arbitrary but are based on scientific methods
- they tell us what poor children actually go without – what makes them different from non-poor children.[1]

2.2 Measuring social exclusion in childhood

Given the current importance of social exclusion in policy terms, there is remarkably little hard evidence about the relationship between poverty and dimensions of social exclusion in childhood. The PSE survey allows the overlap between (severe) child poverty and some possible dimensions of childhood social exclusion – specifically developed as such – to be investigated for the first time. These dimensions include both measures relating directly to children (such as exclusion from school or from social activities) and household-based measures of social exclusion that are likely to impact upon children (such as poor housing or exclusion from financial services).

Although we would not contend that these dimensions are all-encompassing, they provide a starting point for trying to understand 'social exclusion' in childhood and allow the relationship between these measures of social exclusion and severe child poverty to be investigated.

2.3 Issues of definition

For the purposes of Part 1 of the report, a child has been defined as an individual aged 16 or less. The PSE survey provided information on 841 children. The data were then 'weighted' – that is, statistically adjusted so that the findings are representative of the population of all children in Britain, not just those in the survey.

In the PSE survey, questions about children and their circumstances were asked of respondents to the survey. For 95 per cent of children the survey respondent was a parent so that the report refers to parents rather than respondents.

The income data used is net weekly household income and it has been equivalised using an equivalence scale based on budget standards research, which was developed specifically for the survey (see Gordon et al., 2000, for details).

3 Defining severe child poverty

Chapter 1 highlighted the lack of current knowledge regarding children in severe poverty. When severe childhood poverty has been investigated, the most common approach to its definition and measurement has used household income and, conventionally, defines children living in households with incomes in the lowest parts of the income distribution as the most severely poor. This measure, therefore, suffers from all the disadvantages of income poverty measures outlined in the previous chapter.

It was the aim of this part of the project to see if a more useful and illuminating measure of severe child poverty could be found that would clearly discriminate between the experiences of children defined as severely poor and other children. It was decided to explore the range of poverty measures available in the PSE to see which might best contribute to a measure of severe child poverty. In doing so it was felt that the final measure should:

- avoid as many as possible of the disadvantages of income poverty measures
- take into account the child's own experience of poverty or deprivation, not just whether the household as a whole was poor
- measure the parent's experience of poverty or deprivation, separately from that of their children
- consider the income of the household, since the contribution of low household income to the risk of poverty in childhood cannot be ignored.

3.1 Measures of poverty

The three measures of poverty chosen were:
- child deprivation – the child goes without one or more items that the majority of parents in Britain believes to be necessary for children, because parents cannot afford to provide the item(s)
- parent deprivation – the parent goes without two or more items that the majority of adults in Britain believes to be necessary for adults, because the parent cannot afford to provide themselves with the items
- income poverty of the household – the child lives in a household that has less than 40 per cent of median income.

3.1.1 Child's own deprivation
To measure the child's own deprivation, the PSE measure of child deprivation was used because:
- it produces a poverty line specifically related to children, not the household
- the poverty line is not arbitrary, but is based on scientific methods
- it tells us what poor children actually go without – what makes them different from non-poor children.

The last point is of particular importance because it introduces living standards into the measure. If children in households defined as income poor were not going without anything in material (or, indeed, social) terms, then there is no reason why child poverty should be of concern. The measure needs to be able to identify and take into account the impact of income poverty for children in terms of what poor children actually go without that makes their lives worse than those of non-poor children.

The child deprivation measure identified 20 per cent of children as deprived.[1]

3.1.2 Deprivation of their parents

Although child poverty is the central concern both of this report and of current government policy, children's problems will not have been solved if a large proportion of parents remain deprived. Earlier research has shown that households in which children are deprived have to be suffering income poverty to a much greater extent than households in which children are not deprived (Middleton and Adelman, 2003). Parents have to be 'suffering very severe income poverty indeed' to let it impact upon their children. This emphasises the need for a measure of parent's deprivation to be included.[2]

Forty per cent of children were 'poor', in that they had parents who were deprived using this measure.

3.1.3 Income poverty of the household

Household poverty, measured using income, will continue to be at least part of the government's measure of child poverty, not least because of their European Union commitments to do so. (The indicators of poverty and social exclusion endorsed by the Laeken European Council include income measures of poverty (Social Protection Committee, 2001).) In addition, the Government's Public Service Agreement to reduce child poverty by 2004 relies on income poverty measures, as do indicators of progress in *Opportunity for All.*

In addition, a sudden reduction in income will not necessarily be revealed in the deprivation measures of poverty. Even if parents or children were not lacking necessities immediately, it would be anticipated that a period on low income would eventually impact on material deprivation.[3]

The focus of this project is severe child poverty, so the income poverty line needed to be set at a lower level than the usual 60 per cent of median. In addition, to avoid the disadvantage of the usual arbitrary nature of income poverty lines, it was necessary to set an income level that had at least some rational justification. At first, using receipt of Income Support (IS) or means-tested Jobseeker's Allowance (JSA) was considered as a proxy for income poverty. But this would have excluded, by definition, the working poor, and so it was decided to use the income poverty line of below 40 per cent of median equivalised[4] household income before housing costs (see Section 1.4.3) – a poverty line of £107.59 per week. In the total sample of adult respondents, median equivalised household income of recipients of IS or JSA was £106.55 per week, so that our poverty line of 40 per cent of median was similar to the average weekly income of benefit recipients.

Using this measure of income poverty, 17 per cent of children were defined as poor.

3.1.4 Proportion of children in poverty

There were different proportions of children defined as poor using each of the measures described (Figure 3.1).

Figure 3.1 Proportion of children in poverty

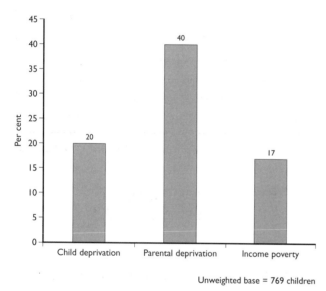

Unweighted base = 769 children

A very much larger proportion of children were in households in which their parents were deprived, than in which the children themselves were deprived, or in which they were income poor. Of course, it was not necessarily the **same** children who were poor on each of the measures. Households may be income poor but yet manage to keep children and/or parents out of deprivation. Or parents and/or children may be deprived but still be in a household with an income of above 40 per cent of the median – as described earlier, 40 per cent of median represents a small amount of weekly income (especially when housing costs still have to be paid).

3.2 Poverty permutations

The difference in the groups of children included in each of the measures is best seen by examining the proportions of children in each of the eight permutations that can be created using these measures (Table 3.1). The majority of children were not poor on any measure (55 per cent). That is, they were not in households that were income poor, nor did they go without one or more necessities themselves (child deprived), nor did their parents lack two or more necessities (parent deprived). Of children who were poor on at least

Table 3.1 Poverty permutations

Column per cent[§]

Poverty permutation	Percentage of children
Poor on no measures:	
Not poor on any measure	55
Poor on one measure:	
Income poor only	2
Child deprivation only	(2)
Parent deprivation only	17
Poor on two measures:	
Income poor and child deprivation	(1)
Income poor and parent deprivation	6
Child and parent deprivation	10
Poor on three measures:	
Income poor, parent and child deprivation	8

Unweighted base = 769 children

§ Column per cent means that each column of the table totals 100 per cent – so, for example, in the above table 55 per cent of children were not poor on any measure, 2 per cent were income poor only and so on (a total of 100 per cent). In other words, all children for whom there are responses are included once, and once only, in the column.

one measure, the greatest proportion had parents who were deprived only – 17 per cent of all children. This confirms the findings of earlier research referred to above, that parents did not have to be particularly poor to go without necessities (Middleton and Adelman, 2003).

The least likely permutations were income poor only, child deprivation only and these two measures combined. In the same research, it was found that poverty had to be very great to let it impact upon the children of the household. Therefore, it would have been surprising to find many children in households where they went without but their parents did not, or in which children went without although the household was not income poor.

3.3 Defining severe child poverty

To determine which of these permutations might best define severe child poverty, the permutations were compared in a number of different ways:
- average income
- the necessities lacked by children and parents
- the number of necessities lacked by both children and parents
- subjective measures of poverty.

3.3.1 Average income
The average equivalised income of children fell into three groups (Table 3.2):

1 **Children not poor on any measure.** Their average income (£354) was significantly higher than all other permutations (with

Table 3.2 **Average income by poverty permutation**

Poverty permutation	Average income per week (£)
Not poor on any measure	354
Income poor only	76
Child deprivation only	(187)
Parent deprivation only	228
Income poor and child deprivation	(79)
Income poor and parent deprivation	69
Child and parent deprivation	217
Poor on all three measures	73
All children	269

Unweighted base = 769 children

the exception of (a) child deprivation only and (b) income poor and child deprivation[5]).

2 **Children who themselves or their parents were deprived but who were not in income poor households (range of average income £187–£228).** The average incomes of these groups of children were significantly lower than those of children not poor on any measure and, in the case of parent deprivation only, significantly higher than children poor on all three measures and children income poor and parent deprived.

3 **Children in income poor households (range of average income £69–£79).** These children had significantly lower average incomes than non-poor children and, in the case of children poor on all three measures and children income poor and parent

deprived, significantly lower average incomes than children who were parent deprived only.

3.3.2 Which necessities were gone without?

CHILDREN

What types of items did children go without because of a lack of money (Table 3.3)? Children who were poor on all three measures were the most likely of all permutations to lack items among those most highly ranked as necessities by all parents in Britain (see Annex A for a full list):

- a warm waterproof coat (13 per cent)
- new properly fitted shoes (17 per cent)
- at least seven pairs of new underpants (18 per cent)
- meat, fish or vegetarian equivalent twice daily (31 per cent)
- fresh fruit and vegetables daily (21 per cent).

There were a few children who went without items, but whose parents did not (child deprived, or income poor and child deprived). This might suggest that parents were putting their own needs before those of their children. However, the items that these children were lacking were generally housing-related and, therefore, particularly difficult and/or expensive to resolve. For example, in both permutations large proportions of children went without a bedroom for every child aged over ten of a different sex.

PARENTS

Children in households poor on all three measures were the most likely to have parents lacking items that were for personal consumption (Table 3.4). For example, among these children there were the highest levels of deprivation for parents of:

- two pairs of all-weather shoes (39 per cent)
- warm waterproof coat (41 per cent)
- outfit for special occasions (40 per cent)
- fresh fruit and vegetables daily (34 per cent).

Parents of children poor on all three measures were no more likely than other parents to lack many of the household items that children will also require (eg, television, beds and bedding, washing machine, medicines). In other words, it appears that children poor on all three measures had parents who were sacrificing their own health and personal well-being by cutting back on food and clothing for the sake of the child, rather than on household items which would affect both parents and children.

However, there were high levels of parental deprivation among housing-related items that would be particularly difficult and/or expensive to resolve for all four groups of children whose parents lacked two or more items. For example, a damp-free home, enough money to keep the home in a decent state of decoration and enough money to replace worn out furniture.

Table 3.3 Items children went without because they could not be afforded

Cell per cent[§]

	Child deprivation only	Income poor and child deprivation	Child and parent deprivation	Poor on all three measures
Three meals a day	0	(11)	(3)	(8)
Toys (eg, dolls, teddies)*	0	0	(1)	(6)
Leisure equipment*	0	(7)	20	18
Bedrooms for every child of different sex over 10 years*	(90)	(21)	(11)	(11)
Warm, waterproof coat	0	0	(11)	(13)
Books of own	0	0	(1)	(1)
Bike: new/second-hand*	0	(23)	24	(15)
Construction toys	0	(17)	(12)	30
Educational games	0	0	24	32
New, properly fitted shoes	(11)	0	(11)	(17)
At least seven pairs of new underpants	0	0	(8)	(18)
At least four jumpers/cardigans/sweatshirts	0	0	16	20
All required school uniform*	0	0	(11)	(16)
At least four pairs of trousers	0	0	18	22
Meat, fish or vegetarian equivalent at least twice a day	0	0	18	31
Fresh fruit and vegetables at least once a day	0	0	(4)	21
Garden to play in	(10)	(29)	(19)	21
Some new, not all second-hand, clothes	0	0	(16)	24
Carpet in bedroom	(5)	(7)	(8)	(9)
A bed and bedding for self	0	0	(5)	(2)

Unweighted base = 224 children (children in these four permutations)

In this analysis, numbers were small and therefore significance tests could not be performed.

* = Age-related items

[§]Cell per cent means that neither the column nor the row adds to 100 per cent. The cell value is simply a free-standing result and it has no relation to the other cells in the column/row. In the above table, in the child deprivation only column, new, properly fitted shoes have a value of 11 per cent – meaning that 11 per cent of children experiencing child deprivation only, lack this item. It has no relationship to the finding that, for example, 10 per cent of the same children lack a garden to play in, or that 11 per cent of children experiencing child and parent deprivation lack new, properly fitted shoes.

Table 3.4 Items parents went without because they could not be afforded

Cell per cent

	Parent deprivation only	Income poor and parent deprivation	Child and parent deprivation	Poor on all three measures
Two meals a day	(1)	0	(3)	(6)
Meat, fish or vegetarian equivalent every other day	(1)	0	(14)	(13)
Heating to warm living areas of the home	(1)	(10)	(5)	(14)
Two pairs of all-weather shoes	(20)	(9)	26	39
Television	0	0	0	(1)
Roast joint or vegetarian equivalent once a week	(3)	(14)	(7)	28
Carpets in living rooms and bedrooms	(1)	0	(19)	(2)
Telephone	(10)	(12)	(3)	(12)
Refrigerator	(2)	0	(1)	(2)
Beds and bedding for everyone	(<0.5)	0	(2)	(3)
Damp-free home	24	(13)	(18)	15
Dictionary	(2)	(3)	(2)	(8)
Presents for friends/family once a year	(5)	(6)	(16)	29
Warm waterproof coat	(10)	(11)	20	41
Washing machine	0	(2)	(3)	(3)
Regular savings (of £10 a month) for rainy days or retirement	72	85	64	89
Money to keep home in decent state of decoration	50	36	64	65
Insurance of contents of dwelling	14	70	25	60
Fresh fruit and vegetables daily	(5)	(4)	(15)	34
An outfit for social occasions	17	(9)	16	40
Deep freeze/fridge-freezer	(1)	0	(10)	(9)
Replace worn out furniture	76	64	82	76
Replace or repair broken electrical goods	28	68	55	70
Appropriate clothes for job interviews	16	(19)	27	26
Medicines prescribed by doctor	(3)	(2)	(6)	(5)
A small amount of money to spend on self weekly not on family	59	60	66	73

Unweighted base = 413 children (children in these four permutations)

In this analysis, numbers were small and therefore significance tests could not be performed.

3.3.3 How many items were lacked?

It is also important to look at the **number** of necessary items that were lacked by children and their parents. The total number of necessities that parents and children could have gone without differed: 26 items for parents and 20 items for children. Therefore, the number of items gone without was turned into a percentage of the total so that the two could be directly compared.

In all but two cases, parents were much more likely to lack items than their children (Figure 3.2), but it was children poor on all three measures who were again the worst off. On average they lacked 17 per cent of items and their parents lacked 29 per cent. These were significantly higher proportions than for the next highest group – children in the child and parent deprived group (12 and 22 per cent of items lacked respectively).

3.3.4 Subjective measures of poverty

Subjective measures of poverty give a guide to how individuals feel about their situation. In the PSE survey a number of questions were asked to try to measure subjective poverty. This analysis focuses on:
- whether parents thought that they were in poverty currently (Table 3.5)
- the extent to which they felt that they had been in poverty in the past (Table 3.6)
- how far they felt they were above or below what they considered to be a poverty line for their family (Table 3.7).

Children who were poor on all three measures had parents who were among the most likely to feel that they were poor at the time of interview all of the time or that they had been in poverty most of the time or often in the past (25 and 24 per cent respectively). Similar figures were found for children who were child and parent deprived (19 and 27 per cent respectively).

Figure 3.2 Proportion of child and parent necessities lacked by poverty

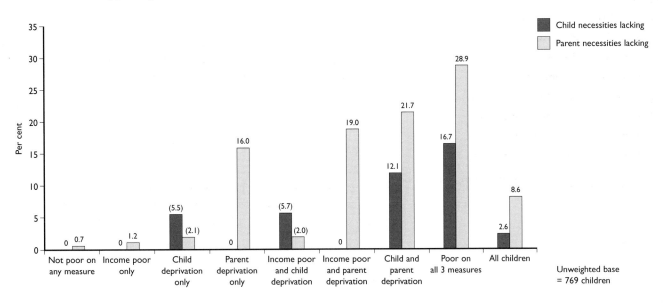

Table 3.5 Poor at the time of interview

Row per cent[§]

	All the time	Sometimes	Never
Not poor on any measure	(1)	13	85
Income poor only	0	(53)	(47)
Child deprivation only	(22)	(44)	(33)
Parent deprivation only	(11)	43	47
Income poor and child deprivation	(13)	(38)	(50)
Income poor and parent deprivation	23	52	(25)
Child and parent deprivation	(19)	54	27
Poor on all three measures	25	60	(15)
All children	8	30	62

Unweighted base = 763 children

[§]Row per cent means that each row of the table totals 100 per cent.
So, in the above table, 8 per cent of all children were poor all of the time,
30 per cent were poor sometimes and 62 per cent were never poor
(a total of 100 per cent).

Table 3.6 How often poor throughout their lives

Row per cent

	Never	Rarely	Occasionally	Often	Most of the time
Not poor on any measure	65	14	14	(6)	(2)
Income poor only	67	(17)	(6)	(11)	0
Child deprivation only	(18)	(27)	(55)	0	0
Parent deprivation only	40	(17)	25	(16)	(3)
Income poor and child deprivation	(56)	(22)	(11)	(11)	0
Income poor and parent deprivation	36	(9)	39	(7)	(9)
Child and parent deprivation	(22)	(7)	44	(21)	(6)
Poor on all three measures	20	(7)	48	(9)	(15)
All children	51	13	23	10	4

Unweighted base = 764 children

Respondents were asked how many pounds per week, after tax, they thought a household like their own would need to be kept out of poverty. They were then asked how far they thought their household was above or below that income level.

Children who were poor on all three measures were the most likely to have parents who reported that they were a lot below their self-defined poverty line – two-thirds of children poor on all three measures (67 per cent). A further fifth of this group had parents who felt that they were a little below that level (19 per cent). However, children in the income poor and parent deprived group and children in the child and parent deprived group were also very likely to have parents who believed they lived below the poverty line for their family – three-quarters of these children lived a little or a lot below their parents' self-defined poverty line (78 and 74 per cent respectively). Children who were not poor on

any measure were by far the most likely to have parents who reported that they lived above the poverty line – two-fifths a lot above that level and just under a third a little above that level.

3.3.5 Definition of severe poverty

The evidence above suggests that severe child poverty can be defined as children who were poor on all three measures of poverty: income poor; child deprived; and parent deprived.[6] This is because they:

- had the lowest average equivalent incomes
- had the highest levels of deprivation of the 'most important' necessities
- lacked the greatest number of necessities – both for parent and child and
- had the highest levels of current subjective poverty.

Therefore, in this part of the report, **severely poor** children will be defined as the 8 per cent of

Table 3.7 How far above or below self-defined income poverty line

Row per cent

	A lot above	A little above	About the same	A little below	A lot below	Don't know
Not poor on any measure	43	30	(2)	7	(6)	12
Income poor only	(12)	(24)	(6)	(24)	(29)	(6)
Child deprivation only	(9)	(36)	0	(9)	(46)	0
Parent deprivation only	(7)	(31)	(9)	(9)	26	18
Income poor and child deprivation	(13)	(13)	(25)	0	(38)	(13)
Income poor and parent deprivation	0	(7)	(5)	(23)	55	(11)
Child and parent deprivation	(14)	(5)	(3)	30	44	(5)
Poor on all three measures	(2)	(4)	(4)	(19)	67	(6)
All children	27	24	4	11	22	12

Unweighted base = 763 children

children who are in this group. Extrapolating this to the whole population of children in Britain would suggest that just over one million children were severely poor in 1999 in that they:

- lived in households which had equivalent incomes below £108 per week
- **and** were deprived of at least one necessary item because it could not be afforded
- **and** had parent(s) who were deprived of two or more necessary items because they could not be afforded.

Non-severe poverty will refer to the group of children who were poor on at least one measure, but less than three. In other words they were included in one of the following groups of children:

- income poor only
- child deprived only
- parent deprived only
- income poor and child deprived
- income poor and parent deprived
- child and parent deprived.[7]

The **no poverty** group will refer to children who were not poor on any measure.

4 Children experiencing severe poverty

This chapter first describes the characteristics of children and their families who were in severe poverty, non-severe poverty and no poverty separately. It then considers all the characteristics together to see which best predicted whether a child would be in severe poverty.

4.1 Characteristics of children in severe poverty

4.1.1 Employment status
Children in severe poverty were very likely to be in a household with no workers. Of children in severe poverty, 82 per cent were in a household with no workers, compared to 24 per cent of children in non-severe poverty and 2 per cent of children not in poverty.

However, a fifth of children in severe poverty were in households where adults were working – half of whose parents were in part-time work. In addition, three-quarters of children in non-severe poverty were in households with workers, two-fifths with two or more workers. This suggests that work does not necessarily prevent poverty, severe or otherwise.

4.1.2 Family type
Children in lone parent families were heavily over-represented in the severe poverty group. They made up two-thirds of children in severe poverty, compared to a population share of just a fifth. Children in lone parent families were also slightly over-represented in the non-severe poverty group and, consequently, under-represented in the no poverty group.

However, children in couple families should not be forgotten. Although just 3 per cent of children in couple households were severely poor (figures shown in Annex B), because of their large population share, they made up 30 per cent of children in severe poverty.

4.1.3 Age of child
Age did not make a significant difference to whether or not a child was in severe poverty, but the age of the **youngest** child in the household did make a significant difference.

However, there does not appear to be a straightforward relationship between the age of the youngest child in the household and poverty status. If anything, it is non-severely poor children who were most different, while severely and non-poor children shared similar proportions in each of the age groups. Children with a youngest child in the household aged 0–1 and 5–10 were more likely to be non-severely poor, children with a youngest child aged 2–4 and 11–16 were more likely to be severely poor or non-poor.

4.1.4 Number of children
The number of children in the household also made a significant difference.

Children in households where they were the only child were over-represented in severe poverty. A quarter of children in severe poverty were only children compared to under a fifth in non-severe or no poverty. In comparison, children in households with one sibling were under-represented in severe poverty (32 per cent) but over-represented in no poverty (57 per cent).

Children in large households were also more likely to be in severe poverty. A fifth of children in severe poverty were in households with four or more children, although they made up just under a tenth of the child population. They were, however, no more likely to be in non-severe poverty.

4.1.5 Ethnic group

Unfortunately, small numbers in the survey meant that ethnicity could only be divided into white and non-white. Over a quarter of children in severe poverty were of non-white ethnicity, whereas the population of non-white children in Britain was just 10 per cent. Looked at another way, this means that over a fifth of non-white children were in severe poverty (figures shown in Annex B). However, non-white children were only slightly over-represented in non-severe poverty (12 per cent) according to their population share, but were slightly under-represented in no poverty (6 per cent).

4.1.6 Tenure

Children in severe poverty were much more likely to live in rented accommodation than children in non-severe poverty and in no poverty. Of the severe child poverty population, around two-fifths lived in local authority rented accommodation and over a third lived in other rented accommodation (housing association or privately rented) – figures around three times greater than their population share. Children in local authority rented accommodation were also over-represented in the non-severe poverty population (28 per cent).

Just 2 per cent of children in owner-occupied homes were severely poor (figures shown in Annex B). However, because of the large proportion of home owners in Britain, 22 per cent of severely poor children lived in owner-occupied homes.

4.1.7 Parental long-standing illness

Children who had at least one parent with a limiting long-standing illness or were in receipt of disability-related benefits were slightly more likely to be in both severe and non-severe poverty than their population share would suggest. Approximately a quarter of children in severe and non-severe poverty had one or more parent with a long-standing illness (25 and 24 per cent respectively), compared to under a fifth of all children (17 per cent). However, these differences were not significant.

4.1.8 Child's long-standing illness

Children with a long-standing illness themselves were no more likely to be in poverty – severe or non-severe.

4.1.9 Household in receipt of Income Support or Jobseeker's Allowance

Unsurprisingly, given the low-income poverty line that has been used in this part of the research, a large majority of children in severe poverty were in households in receipt of Income Support (IS) or Jobseeker's Allowance (JSA) (87 per cent). This leaves 13 per cent of children in severe poverty who were not in receipt of IS or JSA. Presumably these children were receiving household income from elsewhere, from either other benefits or low-paid work.

Table 4.1 Characteristics of children in severe poverty

Column per cent

	No poverty	Non-severe poverty	Severe poverty	All
Employment status***				
Two full-time workers	18	(10)	(2)	14
One full-time, one part-time worker	49	28	(2)	38
One full-time worker	23	21	(6)	21
One or more part-time workers	4	17	(9)	9
More than two workers	(4)	(1)	0	(3)
No workers	(2)	24	82	16
Family type***				
Couple	81	64	30	71
Lone parent	8	28	67	20
Other	11	9	(4)	10
Age of child				
0–1 year	9	13	(6)	10
2–4 years	23	18	26	21
5–10 years	38	45	41	41
11–16 years	30	24	28	28
Age of youngest child in household**				
0–1 year	17	26	(15)	20
2–4 years	32	25	37	29
5–10 years	35	40	35	37
11–16 years	17	9	(13)	14
Number of children***				
1	18	19	24	19
2	57	43	32	50
3	16	31	24	22
4 or more	9	7	20	9
Ethnic group***				
White	94	88	72	90
Non-white	(6)	12	28	10
Tenure***				
Own	90	56	22	72
Rent local authority	(3)	28	42	15
Rent other	7	17	36	13

continued overleaf

Key: Significance – * p<0.05; ** p<0.01; *** p<0.001

Table 4.1 Characteristics of children in severe poverty *continued*

Column per cent

	No poverty	Non-severe poverty	Severe poverty	All
One or more parent has long-standing illness				
No	83	76	76	80
Yes	17	24	25	20
Child has long-standing illness				
No	78	77	85	78
Yes	23	23	(15)	22
Household receiving IS/JSA***				
No	98	73	(13)	82
Yes	(3)	27	87	18
Population size**				
1 million or more	22	26	39	25
100,000 to 999,999	23	27	20	24
10,000 to 99,999	23	28	(19)	25
1,000 to 9,999	18	11	(15)	15
Less than 1,000	14	8	(7)	11
Government office region – grouped				
North	25	23	(20)	24
Midlands	25	21	30	24
South	36	42	35	38
Wales	(6)	8	(4)	7
Scotland	9	5	(11)	8
Highest education level of parent(s)***				
A levels or higher	70	38	23	55
GCE or equivalent	24	34	35	28
CSE or equivalent	(1)	9	(2)	4
None	5	20	40	13

Unweighted base = 729–769 children (variation due to missing values)

Key: Significance – * p<0.05; ** p<0.01; *** p<0.001

Children in non-severe poverty were also more
likely to be in households in receipt of IS or JSA
than all children – a quarter of non-severely poor
children compared to less than a fifth of all
children. However, this means that the majority
of children in non-severe poverty were *not* in
receipt of IS or JSA. This supports the earlier
finding that non-severe poverty exists to a larger
extent in working households (see Section 4.1.1).

4.1.10 Population size[1]

Severe poverty seems to be concentrated in the
most densely populated areas. Two-fifths of
children in severe poverty lived in areas with one
million or more residents, compared to a quarter
of all children. All other, less densely populated
areas were less, or as, likely to have children in
severe poverty than their population share would
suggest. Children in non-severe poverty were
slightly more likely to be living in areas with
fewer residents (100,000 to 999,999 and 10,000
to 99,999): 27 and 28 per cent respectively
compared to 24 and 25 per cent in the all child
population.

4.1.11 Government office region – grouped

Unfortunately, small numbers once again
restricted analysis. The government office regions
of England, Scotland and Wales had to be
combined into just five groups: North, Midlands,
South, Wales and Scotland. Once such groupings
were made there were no significant differences
between these regions/countries. It should be
pointed out that housing costs have not been
taken into account – it may be that, had this
been possible, there would have been significant
differences between the regions.

4.1.12 Highest education level of parent(s)

Children whose parent(s) had a lower level of
education were more likely to be in severe poverty.
Two-fifths of children in severe poverty had
parent(s) without any educational qualifications,
compared to a fifth of children in non-severe
poverty and just one in twenty non-poor
children. However, it should be emphasised that
high education attainment does not necessarily
eradicate poverty. Over a fifth of children in
severe poverty had parent(s) with qualifications
of A level or higher standard, as did almost
two-fifths of children in non-severe poverty.

4.2 Explaining severe poverty[2]

Obviously many of the characteristics in Section
4.1 are related to one another. For example,
children in lone parent households are also likely
to be in households with no workers and to be in
receipt of benefit. Therefore, analysis needs to
untangle these associations to see which are the
most important in predicting whether a child
will be severely poor when all others are taken
into account. The statistical technique used to
do this is 'multinomial regression', and allows
a comparison of each of the characteristics of
non-poor children with non-severely poor and
severely poor children when all other
characteristics are held constant.[3]

Table 4.2 contains only the results from the
analysis that reached statistical significance. In
other words there is only, at most, a 5 per cent
possibility that these results have occurred by
chance. The symbol '+' means that the

characteristic was positively associated with a child being in the poverty group (ie, it increased the risk of poverty). Annex D provides more details about the model, showing the odds ratios for each characteristic (that is, the number of times more or less likely children in each poverty group were to have each significant characteristic).

An example will help to explain Table 4.2. A severely poor child was more likely to be of non-white ethnicity than was a non-poor child. This relationship is independent of the relationship between each of a child's other characteristics and the chance of being in severe poverty. In other words, whether a child was

living in owner-occupied or another type of accommodation, being of non-white ethnicity would still raise the chance (the odds) of severe poverty compared to a child of white ethnicity. In addition, the chances of experiencing each characteristic can be multiplied. So that, for example, for children of non-white ethnicity, living in local authority accommodation would further increase the risk of poverty; the risk would be the odds of being non-white multiplied by the odds of living in local authority accommodation.

The first interesting point to emerge from Table 4.2 is that some of the characteristics identified in earlier paragraphs as associated with severe poverty

Table 4.2 Significant characteristics explaining non-severe and severe poverty

	Compared to a non-poor child:	
	Significant characteristics explaining non-severe poverty	Significant characteristics explaining severe poverty
Part-time workers	+	
No workers	+	+
Non-white ethnicity		+
Local authority accommodation	+	+
In receipt of IS/JSA		+
South	+	+
Midlands		+
Parent has no educational qualifications	+	+
Youngest child aged 0–1	+	
Youngest child aged 5–10	+	

Unweighted base = 714 children

Note: All odds have a significance of at least 95 per cent.

– for example, family type, number of children in the family, population size – have now disappeared. This is not to say that, for example, children in lone parent families were not at risk of severe or non-severe poverty. Rather, it was other characteristics that were commonly present in lone parent families, such as living in local authority accommodation or having no work that explained the poverty, rather than lone parenthood itself.

The characteristics that best predicted whether a child would be severely poor were:
- living in a household with no workers
- living in the South of England
- having parent(s) with no educational qualifications
- living in local authority rented accommodation
- living in a household in receipt of Income Support or Jobseeker's Allowance
- living in the Midlands of England
- being of non-white ethnicity.

The first four of these characteristics also increased the chances that a child would be non-severely poor. However, with the exception of local authority housing, they did so to a lesser extent than for a severely poor child (see Annex D for details). It is clear, therefore, that the chances of being in poverty were increased for children if their parents were not in work, if they lived in the South of England or if their parents had no educational qualifications. However, what made severely poor children different from non-severely poor children was the fact that they were **more** likely to have these characteristics.

In addition, a child in receipt of IS or JSA, a child living in the Midlands and a child of non-white ethnicity had a much higher risk of severe poverty, but not of non-severe poverty. This means that, while non-severely poor children were not different from non-poor children in this respect (when all other characteristics were equal), severely poor children could be identified by their greater propensity to have these characteristics compared to non-poor children. The fact that receipt of IS/JSA remains significant even though worklessness is also included in the model highlights the importance of benefit receipt for experiencing severe poverty. It is not worklessness *per se* that leads to severe poverty, but that children are not protected from the effects of worklessness by an adequate safety net.

5 Poverty and childhood social exclusion

The PSE is the first survey, as far as we are aware, that was specifically designed to attempt to measure and operationalise some possible dimensions of social exclusion in childhood. This is not to say that these dimensions are all-encompassing, the final word on the subject, or even that they add up to something that can be called social exclusion in childhood. They do, however, provide a starting point for examining other aspects of deprivation in childhood outside of material poverty.

The dimensions of social exclusion during childhood included in the PSE are:
- exclusion from social activities
- exclusion from local services
- exclusion during education.

This chapter takes each dimension of social exclusion in turn, describing the measure, highlighting the proportions of children affected and then analysing the degree of overlap between that measure and severe, non-severe and no poverty.

5.1 Poverty and social activities exclusion

Not being able to participate in one or more of a range of social activities, said to be necessary by at least half of parents in Britain, is one possible dimension of social exclusion for children. Studies exploring the minimum needs of children have shown that mothers consider participation in social activities to be vital for children's development (see, for example, Middleton et al., 1994). The large proportions of parents considering the activities in the original children's measure of deprivation to be necessities also suggest the importance that parents place on social participation for their children (see Annex A). Other evidence has pointed to the value children themselves place on being able to participate in activities and clubs (Ridge, 2002).

Parents were asked which of seven activities their children did, which they did not do because they were not wanted and which they did not do because they could not be afforded. Exclusion was defined as not taking part in an activity because it could not be afforded.[1]

Exclusion from activities ranged from 1 per cent of children excluded from a school trip once a term and celebrations on special occasions to 20 per cent excluded from a week's holiday away from home annually (see Figure 5.1 opposite).

5.1.1 How many activities were children excluded from?

A strong relationship between poverty and social activity exclusion was found (Table 5.1). Children

Table 5.1 Mean number of social activities children lacked by poverty status

	Mean number of activities lacking
No poverty	0.13
Non-severe poverty	0.52
Severe poverty	1.74
All children	0.40

Unweighted base = 735 children

Figure 5.1 Social activities children lacked by poverty status

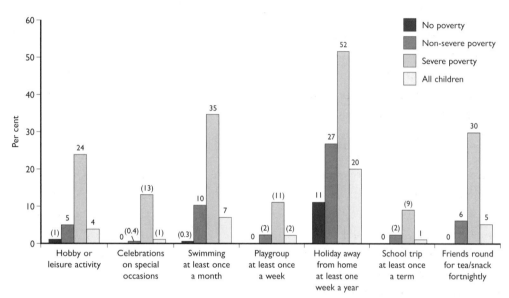

Unweighted base = 742–753 children (variation due to missing values)

in severe poverty on average lacked 1.74 of the seven social activities, a significantly[2] higher level than the other two groups. Non-severely poor children lacked 0.52 activities, a figure three times lower than that of children experiencing severe poverty. In comparison, children that were not in poverty lacked just 0.13 activities or, put another way, on average, 'only' one in eight non-poor children lacked one activity.

5.1.2 Which activities were children excluded from?

An important question is whether the **nature** of social exclusion experienced by children in severe poverty differs from that of non-severely and non-poor children? Do they lack **different activities** or the same activities but to a **greater extent**? This issue was addressed through comparing

the activities that children lacked according to whether they were not in poverty, in non-severe poverty or in severe poverty (Figure 5.1).

It is clear that children in severe poverty were significantly more likely to be excluded from each social activity. In other words, the **manifestation** of exclusion from social activities seemed to be similar for children whatever their poverty status, but the **degree** of exclusion was greater for children in severe poverty.

Compared to children in non-severe poverty, children in severe poverty were much more likely to be excluded from each of the activities. For example, they were five times more likely to be excluded from a hobby or leisure activity and from having friends round for tea fortnightly.

They were approximately twice as likely to have lacked a holiday; half of children in severe poverty went without a holiday. However, children in non-severe poverty also experienced much higher levels of exclusion than non-poor children.

For some families it is probable that choices between activities (and, indeed, items and services) have to be made. For example, they could not afford for their child to attend a leisure activity each week so that the family could afford an annual family holiday. Unfortunately, the data do not allow an analysis of such decisions.

Overall, it is clear that a large proportion of children who were already severely materially deprived and income poor were also excluded from social activities that the majority of parents considered vital to a child's development.

5.2 Poverty and service exclusion

Local services are, potentially, extremely important agents in ameliorating disadvantage, for both areas and individuals – provisions that were once referred to collectively as the 'social wage'. For example, access to a library, bus services and school meals can be seen as promoting social inclusion by benefiting those who could not otherwise afford books, private transport and a healthy diet. This has been recognised by the government's Social Exclusion Unit, which has produced a number of reports on lack of access to services (for example, Department of Health, 1999; Department for Culture, Media and Sport, 1999; Social Exclusion Unit, 2002).

In the PSE, respondents were asked about their use of a range of local public and private services. Six of these were specifically children's services, but the majority of the 'adult' services are also of direct relevance to children (18 out of 20). For each service, respondents were asked whether they:
- used the service and thought it adequate
- used the service but thought it inadequate
- did not use the service because it was not wanted
- did not use the service because it was unavailable or not suitable
- did not use the service because it could not be afforded.

Exclusion here has been defined as either of the latter two – ie, the service was not available (or not suitable) or it could not be afforded.

Levels of service exclusion varied tremendously among the different services. From a positive perspective, exclusion from health services was very low (or non-existent), but 3 per cent of children had parents who reported that they did not have access to a hospital with accident and emergency facilities. Of most concern was the lack of local facilities for children, with 21 per cent excluded from nearby, safe play facilities, 17 per cent from after-school clubs and 15 per cent from youth clubs. Additionally, cultural exclusion from facilities such as the cinema or theatre (17 per cent) or a museum/gallery (18 per cent) was also comparatively high (Table 5.3).

5.2.1 How many services were children excluded from?

Severe poverty was related to service exclusion, with severely poor children being excluded from the highest mean number of the 24 services considered (2.61) (Table 5.2). Non-severely poor children also suffered relatively high levels of service exclusion (1.84). Even non-poor children were not completely immune from service exclusion; on average, they lacked just over one service out of the 24 (1.13). The difference in the levels of service exclusion between the three groups was significant.

Table 5.2 Mean number of local services children went without by poverty status

	Mean number of services lacking
No poverty	1.13
Non-severe poverty	1.84
Severe poverty	2.61
All children	1.51

Unweighted base = 745 children

5.2.2 Which services were children excluded from?

The relationship between poverty and each of the individual services was examined in order to see whether children who were severely poor displayed a different **pattern** or **extent** of service exclusion to children who were non-severely poor or not poor.[3]

For a substantial minority of services (10 out of 24) there was a general trend that severely poor children were more likely to be excluded than non-severely poor children who were, in turn, more likely to be excluded than non-poor children (Table 5.3).[4]

In general, it appeared that the services most likely to be lacked were the same for all children. However, it was apparent that the degree of service exclusion depended upon the severity of poverty. Severely poor children were much more likely to be excluded from leisure activities (sport facilities, play facilities, youth clubs, after-school clubs) than both non-poor and non-severely poor children. At almost equal levels, both severely poor and non-severely poor children were more likely than non-poor children to lack access to a cinema or theatre.

Encouragingly, children in poverty were no more likely to be excluded from the services that might be expected to ameliorate the effects of poverty than were non-poor children. Any findings suggesting that this was not the case would have raised very serious concerns about the effectiveness of public services. Hence, access to education facilities (library, playgroup), health (hospital, doctor, optician) and school-based services (school meals, transport to school) was generally high for nearly all children and not conditional upon their families' financial circumstances or upon their location. Yet some concern must arise from the small numbers who were excluded from these particularly important services.

Table 5.3 Services children lacked by poverty status

Cell per cent

	No poverty	Non-severe poverty	Severe poverty	All children
Library	(1)	(3)	0	(1)
Public sport facilities*	(2)	8	(15)	5
Museum and gallery*	14	24	17	18
Public/village/community hall*	7	14	19	11
Hospital with accident and emergency	(4)	(2)	(6)	3
Doctor	0	0	0	0
Dentist*	0	(2)	(9)	(1)
Optician	(<0.5)	(2)	(2)	(1)
Post office	0	0	0	0
Places of worship	(1)	(1)	0	(1)
Bus services	(4)	(2)	(4)	3
Train/tube station*	(6)	10	22	9
Petrol stations*	(3)	(3)	(11)	3
Chemists*	0	0	(2)	(<0.5)
Corner shop	(7)	(4)	(6)	6
Medium to large supermarket	(1)	(3)	0	(2)
Banks or building societies*	(1)	(2)	(11)	2
Cinema or theatre*	9	27	24	17
Nearby and safe play facilities*	14	28	41	21
School meals	(5)	7	(6)	6
Youth clubs*	12	18	26	15
After-school clubs*	15	17	32	17
Public transport to school	(7)	(5)	(6)	6
Nurseries, playgroups, mother and toddler groups	(4)	(3)	(2)	3

Unweighted base = 757–766 children (variation due to missing values)

Key: * significant difference (p < 0.05)

5.3 Poverty and exclusion during education

The proportion of time that children spend in school means that inclusion during their school life is likely to be vital to their concurrent, and subsequent, inclusion in society. However, children can be excluded from school. As well as direct exclusion by the school, either for a short period (suspension) or entirely (expulsion), exclusion might manifest itself in other ways during school life. The PSE incorporates two possible aspects of exclusion from school life, in addition to suspension from school. These are:

• problems in the school itself due to shortage of resources
• being bullied and/or being accused of bullying.

The government includes the numbers of children suspended from school in its indicators of social exclusion. It has also highlighted the importance of reducing bullying in schools in, for example, the Social Exclusion Unit's report *Schools Plus* (Social Exclusion Unit, 1999). In terms of resource issues, the need to reduce class sizes has been emphasised and funding has also been provided for increasing the number of children with access to computers and the internet in school (see http://www.dfes.gov.uk/ictinschools/).

5.3.1 School resource problems
Parents were asked which, if any, of seven school resource problems their child(ren) had encountered. The problems children were least likely to experience were missing classes because of teacher shortages (5 per cent) and difficulty in obtaining school books (6 per cent) (Figure 5.2).

Children were most likely to have experienced large class sizes of more than 30 pupils (28 per cent).

HOW MANY RESOURCE PROBLEMS WERE EXPERIENCED?
Exclusion from school resources was not related to a child's poverty status: there were no significant differences between the mean number of problems children had depending on whether they were non-poor, non-severely poor or severely poor (Table 5.4). All groups of children experienced, on average, just under one school resource problem. So it would appear that schools are able to provide some protection, at least in terms of resources, against exclusion engendered by poverty.

Previous research exploring the characteristics of children excluded on this measure suggested that any differences in the distribution of school problems was associated with the population density of the area, rather than to poverty. Children in the less densely populated areas were more likely to experience school problems (Adelman et al., 2002). The reasons for this

Table 5.4 Mean number of school problems by poverty status

	Mean number of school problems experienced
No poverty	0.94
Non-severe poverty	0.91
Severe poverty	0.98
All children	0.93

Unweighted base = 760 children

remain speculative, but may be because of the difficulty of providing the full range of resources in smaller schools.

WHICH RESOURCE PROBLEMS WERE EXPERIENCED?

When exploring the relationship between poverty status and each resource issue, severely poor children were found to be significantly more likely to experience 'other resource problems' (just under a fifth of severely poor children) (Figure 5.2). Unfortunately, parents were not asked to specify what these problems were. The only other statistically significant difference between children in the different poverty statuses was for a difficulty in obtaining school books, which was most likely to be experienced by children in non-severe poverty.

Perhaps one of the most revealing findings is that children were as likely to experience large class

sizes whichever poverty status they were in. So, any success that government has had in reducing class sizes is likely to have benefited all children, not just those in poverty.

5.3.2 Bullying[5]

Social exclusion during education could be caused through experiencing bullying or, potentially, through perpetrating bullying. Parents were asked whether or not their children had ever been bullied. Thirty-five per cent of children had parents who reported that their children had been bullied (Figure 5.3). Not surprisingly, far fewer children (just 8 per cent) had parents who reported that their children had ever been accused of bullying.

The parents of severely poor children were significantly more likely to report that their children had been bullied. One half of severely poor children were said to have been bullied,

Figure 5.2 School problems experienced by poverty status

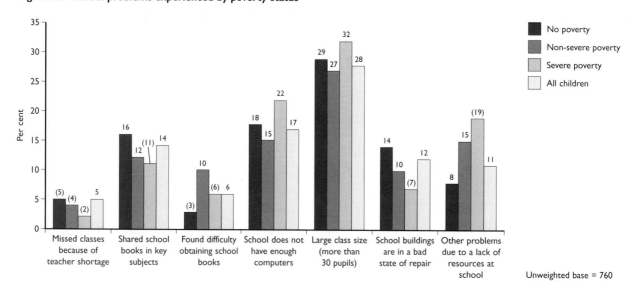

Unweighted base = 760

compared to almost two-fifths of non-severely poor children and less than a third of non-poor children.

The proportion of children accused of bullying, however, was not significantly different between the three groups.

It seems, therefore, that the experience of bullying is particularly likely for severely poor children. Whether this is because their poverty sets them apart from other children within the same school as earlier qualitative research has suggested (Ashworth et al., 1994), or whether bullying is simply more prevalent among severely poor children is unclear. However, the finding that severely poor children were no more likely than children as a whole to be accused of bullying suggests that the former explanation is more likely.

5.3.3 Suspensions[6]
The most obvious form of exclusion during education is when children are suspended from school because of bad behaviour. Just 5 per cent

Figure 5.3 Experiences of suspensions and bullying by poverty status

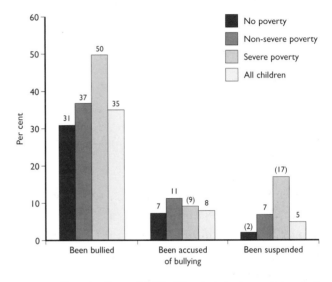

Unweighted base = 728–756 children (variation due to missing values)

of children were reported as ever having been suspended from school (Figure 5.3). Severely poor children were significantly more likely to have been suspended from school – they were over twice as likely to have been suspended as non-severely poor children and over eight times more likely than non-poor children.

6 Poverty and household exclusion

There are forms of exclusion that affect the whole household, not just the children, and from which parents are largely unable to protect their children. The PSE identified four areas of potential exclusion at the household/parental level that are also likely to impact on children:
- poor housing quality
- poor local neighbourhood
- financial exclusion
- poor parental emotional well-being.

Once again, it is unlikely that these are the only household/parental exclusion experiences that will impact upon children. However, they provide a starting point in allowing a comparison of the exclusion experiences of (severely) poor children and non-poor children.

Following the format of the previous chapter, this chapter takes each exclusion measure in turn, describing the measure, highlighting the proportions of children affected and then analysing the degree of overlap between the measure and severe, non-severe and no poverty.

6.1 Housing quality

Housing quality is clearly of vital importance for a child's well-being and is the only environment-based indicator of social exclusion specifically for children and young people in *Opportunity for All*: 'a reduction in the proportion of children who live in a home that falls below the set standard of decency'.

A range of questions was available from the PSE about the quality of the respondent's housing:
- the state of repair of their home
- specific problems with their accommodation
- any relationship between poor health and their housing.

6.1.1 State of repair of home
There were stark differences in the reported state of repair of the homes of poor children and non-poor children (Figure 6.1). Three-quarters

Figure 6.1 State of repair of housing by poverty status

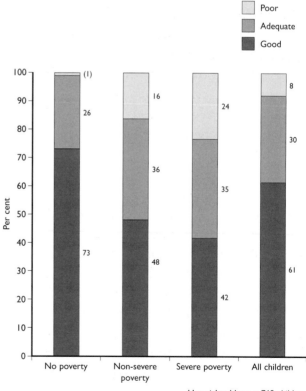

Unweighted base = 769 children

(73 per cent) of non-poor children lived in homes described as in good repair, compared to just over two-fifths of severely poor children and almost a half of non-severely poor children (42 and 48 per cent respectively).

Differences between severely and non-severely poor children were less stark, but still in evidence. Although, just over a third of both severely and non-severely poor children lived in homes perceived to be in adequate repair, almost a quarter of severely poor children lived in 'poor' housing, compared to a sixth of non-severely poor children.

6.1.2 Problems with accommodation
The PSE also asked respondents whether or not they had each of a number of specific problems with their accommodation. As with the state of repair of their homes, there were stark differences between poor and non-poor children, yet few between severely and non-severely poor children.

HOW MANY PROBLEMS WERE EXPERIENCED?
Adding together the number of problems that children had with their accommodation as a proxy for severity of housing conditions showed that children in severe and non-severe poverty were likely to experience an average of 1.38 and 1.31 housing problems respectively, a non-significant difference (Table 6.1). These figures were, however, significantly greater than the average of 0.49 problems experienced by non-poor children.

Table 6.1 Mean number of housing problems by poverty status

	Mean number of housing problems experienced
No poverty	0.49
Non-severe poverty	1.31
Severe poverty	1.38
All children	0.87

Unweighted base = 769 children

WHICH PROBLEMS WERE EXPERIENCED?
In many cases, severely and non-severely poor children were almost as likely to experience a problem as each other, and both were always far more likely to experience the problem than were non-poor children, with the exception of 'other' problems (Table 6.2). Of non-poor children, 59 per cent experienced none of the housing problems compared to only 28 per cent of children in non-severe poverty and 24 per cent of children in severe poverty. Severely poor children were the most likely to have experienced living in a home that was too dark and in one with shortage of space. However, non-severely poor children were the most likely to have a leaky roof and damp walls or floors.

6.1.3 Health and housing
PSE respondents were asked whether their own health, or the health of anyone in the household, had been made worse by their housing situation. Once again it appears that, while the differences between non-poor and poor children (both severe

Table 6.2 Housing problems by poverty status

Cell per cent

	No poverty	Non-severe poverty	Severe poverty	All children
Shortage of space	23	40	54	32
Too dark, not light enough	(1)	7	(13)	4
Lack of adequate heating	(3)	15	15	9
Leaky roof	(1)	(11)	(2)	5
Damp walls, floors, foundations etc.	(3)	18	(13)	9
Rot in window frames or floors	(7)	16	(17)	11
Mould	(3)	14	(13)	8
No place to sit outside e.g. a garden or terrace	(1)	7	(9)	4
Other	(6)	(4)	(4)	5
None of these problems	59	28	24	44

Unweighted base = 769 children

and non-severe) were substantial, the differences between severely and non-severely poor children were, although still in evidence, somewhat smaller (Table 6.3). The health of someone in the household was reported to have been made worse by their housing situation for just 2 per cent of children not in poverty compared with 15 and 9 per cent of children in severe and non-severe poverty respectively.

Table 6.3 Health made worse by housing situation by poverty status

	Proportion of children whose health or health of someone in household was made worse by housing situation
No poverty	(2)
Non-severe poverty	9
Severe poverty	(15)
All children	6

Unweighted base = 767 children

6.2 Quality of the local neighbourhood

The quality of the neighbourhood in which a child lives is largely out of the control of parents but may have a major impact on children's experiences as they grow up. Once again, the government has recognised the importance of the local neighbourhood in terms of increasing or decreasing the chances of experiencing some forms of social exclusion, including that of children. In its consultation document *Measuring Child Poverty* it is noted that

> '...(apart from income) other influences also matter, such as neighbourhood environments... Those living in poorer neighbourhoods often have to put up not only with a rundown physical environment, but also the worst public services...'
>
> Department for Work and Pensions, 2002b, p.10

The PSE included a number of questions concerning the quality of the local area in which respondents lived:

- satisfaction with the area
- problems experienced in the area.

6.2.1 Satisfaction with area

Children in severe poverty were three times as likely as children in non-severe poverty to live in areas with which parents were slightly or very dissatisfied (a total of 41 per cent compared to 13 per cent) (Figure 6.2). In addition, children in severe poverty were over three times less likely to live in areas with which parents were very satisfied (13 per cent) compared to children in non-severe poverty (47 per cent).

The quality of the neighbourhoods of children in non-severe poverty was lower than that of neighbourhoods where non-poor children lived. Children in non-severe poverty were twice as likely to live in areas with which parents were dissatisfied (13 per cent compared to 8 per cent) and significantly less likely to live in areas of high satisfaction (47 per cent compared to 64 per cent).

6.2.2 Problems with the area

Respondents were asked whether their area suffered from each of 14 problems (see Table 6.5 overleaf).

HOW MANY PROBLEMS WERE EXPERIENCED?
On average, children as a whole experienced just over two of the problems in their area (Table 6.4). Severely poor children experienced a significantly higher average number of problems (4.83) than non-severely and non-poor children, and

Figure 6.2 Satisfaction with area by poverty status

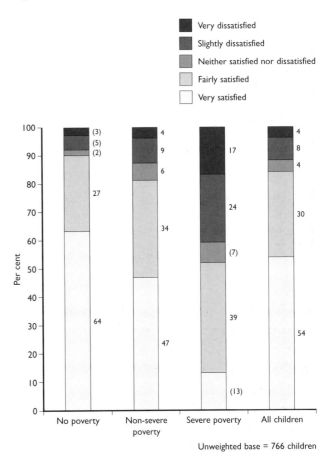

Unweighted base = 766 children

Table 6.4 Mean number of problems with area by poverty status

	Mean number of common problems with area experienced
No poverty	1.59
Non-severe poverty	2.94
Severe poverty	4.83
All children	2.34

Unweighted base = 766 children

non-severely poor children experienced significantly more problems than non-poor children (averages of 2.94 and 1.59 respectively).

WHICH PROBLEMS WERE EXPERIENCED?
Just a quarter of all children had parents who experienced none of the 14 area problems (26 per cent) (Table 6.5). The most commonly reported problems were teenagers hanging around on the street and dogs and dog mess, both reported by the parents of two-fifths of children. A quarter experienced rubbish or litter lying around and/or a risk from traffic for pedestrians or cyclists.

The likelihood of experiencing these area problems was greatest for children in severe poverty. Just one in 16 children in severe poverty (6 per cent) did not experience any of the problems compared to one in seven non-severely poor children (14 per cent), and one in three non-poor children (36 per cent). With only a couple of exceptions, children in severe poverty were the most likely to have parents who reported each of the problems. Three-quarters lived in neighbourhoods that had problems with teenagers hanging around on the streets. Over a half of children in severe poverty had parents who

Table 6.5 Problems with area by poverty status

Cell per cent

	No poverty	Non-severe poverty	Severe poverty	All children
Noisy neighbours or loud parties	8	20	54	16
Graffiti on walls and buildings	(3)	12	19	7
Teenagers hanging around on the streets	28	50	76	40
Homeless people and/or people begging	(1)	(2)	(4)	(2)
Rubbish or litter lying around	16	29	56	24
Dogs and dog mess	34	47	56	40
Homes and gardens in bad condition	8	18	35	14
Vandalism and deliberate damage to property	11	22	35	17
Insults or attacks to do with someone's race or colour	(2)	9	(11)	5
Poor street lighting	7	10	33	10
Street noise (eg, traffic, businesses, factories)	9	17	32	13
Pollution, grime or other environmental problems caused by traffic or industry	9	14	20	12
Lack of open public places	(3)	12	(19)	8
Risk from traffic for pedestrians or cyclists	22	31	35	26
No area problems	36	14	(6)	26

Unweighted base = 766 children

commonly experienced problems with dogs and dog mess, rubbish or litter lying around and noisy neighbours or loud parties. A third had problems with homes and gardens in bad condition, vandalism and deliberate damage to property, poor street lighting, street noise and risk from traffic for pedestrians or cyclists.

For children in non-severe poverty, experiences of these problems were much more common than for non-poor children. In many cases, they were over twice as likely as children not in poverty to experience the problems. So, for example, half of non-severely poor children had parents who said that their neighbourhood experienced problems with dogs and dog mess, and half also had parents who reported neighbourhood problems with teenagers hanging around on the streets. In addition, a third had parents who reported neighbourhood problems with rubbish or litter lying around, while over a fifth had problems with noisy neighbours or parties, and with vandalism and deliberate damage to property.

6.3 Financial exclusion

'Financial exclusion' is a term used here to describe a situation in which people do not have access to mainstream financial services and/or in which household financial problems are brought about by such lack of services or simply by low income. The Social Exclusion Unit has paid a great deal of attention to this topic, with two reports by the Policy Action Teams being published in the lifetime of the Unit: *Initiatives to Tackle Financial Exclusion* (HM Treasury, 1999a)

and *Access to Financial Services* (HM Treasury, 1999b).

The PSE asked respondents a number of questions about their use of financial services and financial problems they experienced. For this analysis the following questions were used. Respondents were asked whether they had:
* been in debt
* access to a bank or building society account
* borrowed money
* been disconnected from the main utilities
* used less of the main utilities because of a lack of money.

6.3.1 Debt
As an indicator of debt, respondents were asked whether they had been seriously behind with the payment of certain bills in the last 12 months, including main utilities, housing costs, loans, credit cards and so on.

Children in severe poverty were most likely to have parents who had experienced debt in the last 12 months, a figure of almost two-thirds (65 per cent) (Figure 6.3, overleaf). However, debt was clearly also a problem for the parents of children in non-severe poverty. Over two-fifths of non-severely poor children had parents who were seriously behind with their bill payments (45 per cent). This compared to just one in 16 non-poor children (7 per cent).

6.3.2 Bank or building society account
The PSE asked about access to two financial services. First, the list of necessary items for adults included insurance for home

Figure 6.3 Dimensions of financial exclusion by poverty status

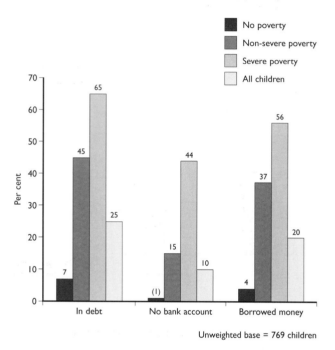

Unweighted base = 769 children

contents. Section 3.3.2 has already shown the large proportion of severely poor children whose parents could not afford home contents insurance (60 per cent). This measure cannot be used in the analysis here because it has already been used in the severe poverty definition.

Secondly, respondents were asked whether they, their partner (if applicable), or both of them had a bank or building society account, or not. These responses were combined to determine whether or not any adult in the household had an account.

In total, 10 per cent of children lived in households where their parents did not have access to a bank or building society account (Figure 6.3). Of non-poor children, just 1 per

cent had parents without access to a bank or building society account; this rose to 15 per cent of non-severely poor children, but to 44 per cent of severely poor children.

6.3.3 Borrowing money

Another dimension of financial exclusion could be having to borrow money from sources other than a bank or building society, such as from pawnbrokers, money lenders or family and friends. Respondents to the PSE were asked whether they had borrowed money from sources other than a bank or building society in the past year in order to pay for their day-to-day needs.

In total, a fifth of all children lived in households in which money had been borrowed (Figure 6.3). However, once again, the rates of borrowing varied tremendously depending on poverty status. Just one in 25 non-poor children (4 per cent) lived in households that had borrowed money compared with almost two-fifths of non-severely poor children (37 per cent). For severely poor children, the proportion was 50 per cent higher again, at almost three-fifths of children (56 per cent).

6.3.4 Utilities

Apart from being behind with bills, financial problems might also lead to households cutting back, perhaps to detrimental levels, on the utilities that they use, in order to reduce their bills. Furthermore, severe financial difficulties could lead to non-payment of bills and to one or more of the essential utilities being cut off. The PSE asked which utilities (water, gas, electricity and telephone) respondents had ever used less of because they could not be afforded and which they had ever been disconnected from as a result of non-payment of bills.

Just under a fifth of all children lived in households that had cut back on the amount of utilities that they used (19 per cent) (Figure 6.4). However, the proportions who had cut back were very different according to poverty status. Just 3 per cent of non-poor children were in households that had cut back their use of the utilities compared with 32 per cent of non-severely poor children. However, for severely poor children the proportion was double that of the non-severely poor; 65 per cent of severely poor children had parents who had cut back their use of utilities.

Poor children were much more likely than non-poor children to live in a household that had experienced a disconnection from at least one of the utilities. While only one in 100 (1 per cent) of non-poor children were in households that had been disconnected, around a fifth of children in non-severe poverty and a quarter of children in severe poverty had actually been disconnected from at least one of the utilities (Figure 6.4).

6.4 Emotional well-being

It is well established that poverty can lead to poor mental health or depression[1] (see, for example, Weich and Lewis, 1998; Payne, 2000), suggesting that children in poverty will be more likely to experience living with parents with impaired mental well-being. The government has identified

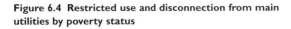

Figure 6.4 Restricted use and disconnection from main utilities by poverty status

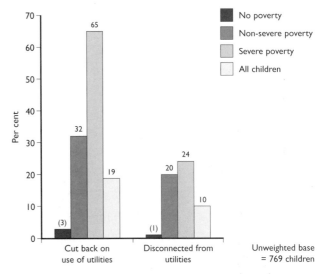

individuals with mental health problems as among those prone to risk of social exclusion (Social Exclusion Unit, 2001). In 2003, the Social Exclusion Unit began a project 'to address the barriers to opportunity faced by adults with mental health problems' (http://www.social exclusionunit.gov.uk/mental_health/mental_ health.htm).

PSE respondents were asked 12 questions designed to measure mental well-being. The questions included their views on how they felt about their ability to overcome difficulties, to make decisions, to face up to problems and so on. For each question answers ranged from one (more capable than usual) to four (much less capable than usual). These scores were summed to give a total general health questionnaire (GHQ) score, therefore the higher the score the worse an individual's mental well-being. The best (lowest) score possible is 12 – scoring one on each question, the worst (highest) score is 48 – scoring four on each question.

The average GHQ score rose significantly as the severity of poverty increased, with average scores of 22.28 for non-poor children, 25.16 for non-severely poor children and 27.78 for severely poor children (Figure 6.5). We cannot here explore the consequences for children of their parents' poor mental health (this would require longitudinal data). However, it seems likely that, rather than the parents of poor children being able to provide a positive support mechanism for their children to help ameliorate the material hardships of poverty, the reverse is likely to be true.

Figure 6.5 Average GHQ score of parent by poverty status

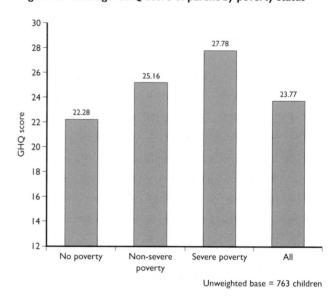

Unweighted base = 763 children

7 Summary of key findings

This part of the report had two main aims:

1 to find a new way of measuring severe child poverty that goes beyond one-dimensional income-based definitions of poverty so that the measure can describe, and take into account, the material deprivation experienced by poor children and their parents

2 to examine the relationships between severe child poverty and some possible dimensions of social exclusion in childhood.

7.1 Definition and measurement

Using the PSE, child income poverty and deprivation was measured using a combination of three definitions:
- the child's own deprivation – children going without one or more 'necessities' because they could not be afforded
- the deprivation of their parents – parents going without two or more 'necessities' because they could not be afforded
- the income poverty of their household – household with an income of below 40 per cent of median.

Children were defined as those aged 16 years or less.

The three poverty measures created eight poverty permutations:
- not poor on any measure
- income poor only
- child deprivation only

- parent deprivation only
- income poor and child deprivation
- income poor and parent deprivation
- child and parent deprivation
- poor on all three measures.

Children were defined as being in severe poverty if they were poor on all three measures. This was because children in this group:
- had the lowest average incomes
- were most likely to lack the 'most important' necessities
- lacked the greatest number of necessities – both adult and child
- had the highest levels of current subjective poverty.

Using this definition, **8 per cent of British children – approximately one million – were severely poor and 37 per cent non-severely poor** (poor on one or two of the three measures).

7.2 Which children were in severe poverty?

Both severely poor children and non-severely poor children could be identified by the following characteristics (when all other characteristics were taken into account):
- living in a household with no workers
- living in the South of England
- having parents with no educational qualifications
- living in local authority rented accommodation.

However, severely poor children were more likely to have the first three of these characteristics than non-severely poor children.

In addition, severely poor children were much more likely to have three other characteristics that distinguished them from non-poor children, and which did not identify non-severely poor children. These were:
- living in a household receiving Income Support or Jobseeker's Allowance
- living in the Midlands of England
- being of non-white ethnicity.

7.3 Which children were socially excluded?

The PSE includes three areas that might indicate social exclusion in childhood:
- exclusion from social activities
- exclusion from local services
- exclusion during education.

The data also include household and parental measures of social exclusion that are likely to have an impact on children and which parents may find particularly difficult to remedy. These were identified as:
- exclusion through poor housing quality
- exclusion through poor neighbourhood quality
- financial exclusion
- exclusion through poor parental mental well-being.

With a few exceptions, social exclusion was strongly associated with severe poverty. On all of

the dimensions studied, there was no apparent difference in the **pattern** of exclusion whether the child was not poor, non-severely poor, or severely poor. Rather, in general, the greater the severity of poverty, the greater the number of individual services/activities from which a child was excluded or the greater the number of problems the child experienced. In other words, severe poverty does not lead to a different **form** of exclusion to that experienced by non-poor or non-severely poor children, rather it is different in its **degree**. Severely poor children were, quite simply, excluded from a greater number of services/ activities, or experienced a greater number of problems, than non-severely poor and non-poor children.

For example:
- The rate of being unable to afford to participate in children's social activities was much higher among severely poor children than among their non-severe poor and non-poor counterparts. The average non-participation rate for severely poor children was 25 per cent compared to 7 per cent for non-severely poor children and just 2 per cent for non-poor children.
- Severely poor children were more likely to be excluded from local services – either because they could not be afforded or accessed. Of severely poor children, 11 per cent were excluded compared with 8 per cent for non-severely poor children and 5 per cent for non-poor children.
- Severely poor children were more likely to experience problems with their local area. Of severely poor children, 35 per cent

experienced problems with their local area compared with 21 per cent of non-severely poor children and 11 per cent of non-poor children.

In terms of the quality of their housing, both severely and non-severely poor children were much more likely to experience poor housing quality than non-poor children. Housing problems were experienced by 16 per cent of severely poor children and 14 per cent of non-severely poor children compared with 6 per cent of non-poor children.

Part 2 Persistence of severe child poverty

8 Introduction

This part of the report uses an income measure of severe child poverty to track children's poverty experiences over a number of years; in particular, to analyse the **persistence** of severe poverty for children.

This chapter summarises, first, the advantages of analysing poverty over time, and the ways in which the persistence of child poverty has been measured previously. It then describes the data used in this report, taken from the British Household Panel Survey, and the method by which the sample of children for this analysis was developed. Finally, the measure of severe child poverty used in this part of the report is described, paying particular attention to differences between this measure and that used in Part 1 of the report.

Chapter 9 describes the poverty transitions made by children between severe poverty, non-severe poverty and no poverty over a five-year period and sets out the proportions of children in each of these groups. It goes on to develop a categorisation of persistent and severe child poverty, and investigates the length of time children spent in each poverty state and, if they moved poverty state, to where they moved. Chapter 10 investigates a range of characteristics of children and their families in persistent and severe poverty and explores which of these

characteristics potentially best explain why they were in this state. As in Part 1, the analysis then considers the overlaps between poverty and some possible measures of social exclusion, in terms of household exclusion (Chapter 11), parent's experiences of exclusion (Chapter 12) and, finally, young people's own experiences of exclusion (Chapter 13). Chapter 14 provides a summary of the key findings.

8.1 Analysing poverty over time

If the proportion of children in poverty can be measured at a point in time, why should we be concerned with the proportion of children in poverty over a period of time? Bradbury et al., (2001) identified five reasons which neatly summarise the importance of analysing child poverty dynamically:

- Past poverty is likely to have an adverse affect on the current living standards of a child.
- It is possible to establish whether poverty is experienced by a small number of children (the same children being poor at each point in time) or whether it is experienced by different children (different children being poor at each point in time).
- There is evidence that the impact of child poverty in adulthood depends upon the length of time spent in poverty during childhood.

- By focusing on movements into and out of poverty, it is possible to identify what triggers these movements. In other words it is possible to gain an understanding of what leads to a move into or out of poverty.
- Poverty reduction policies can be designed appropriately to deal with the changing, or stable, nature of the poverty population.

8.2 Measuring persistent child poverty

Earlier research on persistent child poverty in the UK was limited by the lack of suitable data recording children's experiences over time. The availability of the British Household Panel Survey (described in greater detail in Section 8.3) has made it possible to begin to explore British children's experiences of poverty over time (see for example, Hill and Jenkins, 2001; Ermisch et al., 2001).

8.2.1 The 'official measure' of persistent poverty

A reduction in the extent of persistent low income is one of the government's indicators of progress for children (and working age and older people) in its annual poverty report, *Opportunity for All*. People in persistent low income are defined as those living in households with low incomes in any three out of four consecutive years. Figures based on two 'poverty lines' are given: one for 60 per cent of median income and another for 70 per cent of median income, both based on before housing costs income. Between 1994–1997 and 1997–2000, the trend in persistent child poverty was constant: 16 per cent of children had

incomes below 60 per cent of the median in three of the previous four years and 26 per cent of children had income below 70 per cent of the median in three of the previous four years (Department for Work and Pensions, 2002a).

8.2.2 Persistent severe poverty

The government's official measure does not take into account persistent **severe** poverty, that is, children who remain in the deepest poverty for long periods of time. This is hardly surprising since there has been little research at all on severe child poverty, as highlighted in Chapter 1. However, it is extremely important to understand both persistent and severe poverty in order to determine whether it is children at the very bottom of the income distribution who are also most likely to be persistently poor. This question has important policy implications. For example, if severe poverty and persistent poverty are experienced by different groups of children, it is important to establish whether the processes, hence the likely policy solutions, that underlie severe poverty are the same as those that create persistent poverty. However, if severe poverty is also persistent, it is necessary to determine what processes appear to underlie this that differ from non-persistent and non-severe poverty.

8.3 The data

The British Household Panel Survey (BHPS) is the only British survey that collects information from a nationally representative sample of people in private households who are followed over an extended period of time. Consequently, it is the best source of British data with which to measure poverty persistence. The BHPS started in 1991 with a representative sample of 5500 households (13,840 household members). Since that time, individuals aged 16 or over in these households have been re-interviewed every year, the most recent data being for 2001/2 (Wave 11). The survey includes information about households, respondent individuals and children, and since 1994 has also included a Youth Questionnaire asked of all children aged 11 to 15.

8.3.1 Income data

The survey collects gross income data (that is, before the deduction of direct tax and occupational pension contributions). However, for poverty analysis it is often advantageous to use net income.[1] A team at the Institute for Social and Economic Research has estimated current net weekly income[2] for households in the BHPS from Wave 1 to Wave 9 (1991–1999). Therefore net income data from these years have been analysed in this report. These net income data were up-rated to 1999 price levels so that poverty could be defined in relation to the income measure collected in the Poverty and Social Exclusion Survey of Britain (PSE), which was also undertaken in 1999 (see Section 8.4 for the definition of poverty used in this part of the report).[3] The net income data have been equivalised using the PSE equivalence scale and are before housing costs. When income is referred to in what follows, it should be taken to mean net weekly equivalised income before housing costs.

8.3.2 Children included in the sample

Children have been defined as those aged 0–19 years, rather than 0–16 years, as in Part 1. The age range has been extended to ensure that the 'phases' of childhood used in the analysis (see below) correspond approximately to major changes in a child's life in relation to formal education, and to capture policy concerns with the post-16 outcomes for children from poorer families. In addition, the extended age range provided a sufficiently large sample of children for the analysis.

Two data challenges had to be overcome to create a sample that allowed an analysis of persistent child poverty. First, the BHPS has not been in existence for long enough to follow a group of children through the whole of their childhood. With only nine waves (years) of data, for example, children who were less than one year old in the first wave of data collection will only have reached eight years of age by the ninth wave. Secondly, there is the problem of sample size. Only 204 children were less than one year old in the first wave of interviews for the BHPS. Since some families inevitably drop out of the survey between waves of interviews, substantially fewer than 204 would still be in the sample after 16 years, that is, when children had 'completed' their childhood.

In response to these challenges, for this analysis 'phases' of childhood were chosen by the authors, with two considerations governing the definition of these phases. First, it was important to ensure that each phase was of equal length so that poverty persistence would be measured over an equal number of years for each age group. Secondly, it was important that these phases should correspond roughly to sociologically meaningful periods of a child's life. After some initial explorations, four phases of childhood were defined: 0–4 years, 5–9 years, 10–14 years and 15–19 years. These phases correspond approximately to pre-school, primary school, intermediate (pre-exam) schooling, and examination years and post-compulsory schooling. Each phase encompassed five years of a child's life and, therefore, each child was included in the analysis for just these five years.

Children could only be included in the sample once and once only. They were followed from 1991 to 1995, or from 1992 to 1996, and so on up to the date range 1995 to 1999 (ie, each child was followed over a five-year period). Each child was introduced to the sample when he or she was less than 1 year old, 5 years old, 10 years old or 15 years old (ie, over the appropriate phase of childhood). (See Annex F for more details regarding the construction of the cohorts and the consequences that they may have for understanding recent policy.) Children in each of the four chilhood phases – or cohorts – were combined to create a single sample of 2130 children.[4] The data presented in the following chapters have been weighted to be representative of the population of children in Britain.[5]

8.4 Definition of severe poverty

The BHPS contains detailed income information and also a number of measures that might be seen as capturing some dimensions of social exclusion (see Chapters 11–13). However, it does not include the same set of deprivation indicators available in the PSE on which the definition of severe poverty in Part 1 relied, so that the definition of severe poverty in Part 2 has

relied solely on an income measure of poverty. Nevertheless, in order to make the findings from Part 1 and Part 2 as comparable as possible, it was important to be as consistent as possible with the approach to defining severe poverty.

Exploratory analysis, which investigated a number of options, suggested that for maximum comparability the poverty levels for the BHPS analysis should be set at the **median** income levels of the severe and non-severe poverty groups as defined in the PSE analysis. Consequently, in Part 2 of the report, the poverty groups are as follows:
- severe poverty – household income below 27 per cent of median household income
- non-severe poverty – household income between 27 and 59 per cent of median household income
- no poverty – household income above 59 per cent of median household income.

8.4.1 Monetary value of the severe poverty definition

In the BHPS, at 1999 prices, these proportions of median income correspond to a severe income poverty line of £64.46 and a non-severe poverty line of £140.86 (remembering that this income is equivalised household income before housing costs). Using prices for the first quarter of 2003, these incomes would be equivalent to £70.26 and £153.54, respectively. In both 1999 and 2003, these monetary values of the severe income poverty line were somewhat lower than (equivalised) Income Support levels depending on family type and the year under consideration (see Annex G for details). This inevitably raises the question why any children should have had incomes below the Income Support level between 1991 and 1999. There are at least five possible reasons: very low wages, non take-up of benefits, non-entitlement to benefit (because savings were too high, for example), deductions from benefits at source (to repay Social Fund loans, for example), and possible errors in reporting or recording income data.

8.4.2 Differences between the two measures of severe poverty

It is important to make clear that because of the different (severe) poverty definitions used in Part 1 and Part 2 of the report, there are some differences in the proportions of children in poverty using the two measures. Using the PSE data, Table 8.1 shows the proportion of children in each of the poverty groups using the PSE income and deprivation definition of poverty and this current (income only) definition. Applying the income only measure to the PSE data results in a much lower proportion of children in non-severe poverty than using the PSE definition of non-severe poverty (22 per cent compared to 37 per cent). The proportion of children in severe poverty is the same using both definitions (8 per

cent). However, it is important to note that not all children will be in the same poverty group under each definition (see Annex H).

8.4.3 When children are in poverty

The measure of income used in the analysis that follows is current net weekly household income. So what is actually being measured is whether or not children were in severe, non-severe or no poverty in the week of interview in each of the five years they are in the sample. Weekly incomes will obviously fluctuate for some households between different weeks of the year, so not all those who ever experienced (severe) poverty will necessarily be captured in our analysis. Conversely it is possible, if unlikely, that children who were measured as being in severe poverty in that week in each of the five years might not have been in severe poverty at all for the remaining 51 weeks of each year. In summary, this definition captures children who have experienced (severe) poverty at a particular point in the year and who did so over a number of years. Although this is subject to measurement error, as is any other measure of poverty, it has the virtue that it uses the same approach as is used in the official measure of poverty persistence (see Section 8.2.1).

Table 8.1 Proportion of children in poverty using two poverty definitions

Column per cent

Poverty state	Income and deprivation measure	Income only definition
No poverty	55	70
Non-severe poverty	37	22
Severe poverty	8	8

9 Children in persistent and severe poverty

This chapter explores the poverty status of children using the first nine waves of the BHPS and develops a categorisation of the severity and persistence of poverty based on children's experiences of poverty during the five-year period in which each child was included in the analysis (see Section 8.3.2 and Annex F for details). The chapter also examines the length of time that children spent in severe, non-severe and no poverty and, for those children who moved between these poverty states, which states they moved between.

9.1 Children in severe poverty

The proportion of children in severe poverty (ie, with an income below 27 per cent of median household income) in each year ranged from a low of 2 per cent to a high of 5 per cent, with a mode of 4 per cent (Table 9.1). Whilst this is a relatively small proportion of children overall, these figures translate roughly as between a little over a quarter and just under three-quarters of a million children aged 19 and under[1] being severely poor in each year in the 1990s.

The proportion of children in non-severe poverty (ie, in households with an income between 27 and 59 per cent of median household income) also varied from year to year, from 21 to 29 per cent. The figures show a steep decline in non-severe poverty, particularly between 1996 and 1997. By contrast, for severe poverty a decline occurred between 1991 and 1996, but by 1999 seemed to have risen back to the 1991 high of 5 per cent (although sample sizes were small in 1991 and 1999).

However, these figures are just 'point in time' measures of poverty and this phase of the research is more concerned with the **length of time** children spent in (severe) poverty. It is to this that we now turn.

9.2 Children in persistent and severe poverty

In each of the five years that children were observed they could be in severe or non-severe poverty or not in poverty (no poverty). Comparing the sequence of patterns of these three states over five years produced 21 different 'poverty persistence' permutations (see Annex I for the proportions in each of these permutations). These permutations were collapsed to form five

Table 9.1 Proportion of children in severe and non-severe poverty 1991–1999

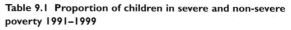

Row per cent

	Proportion of children in:		
	Severe poverty	**Non-severe poverty**	**No poverty**
1991	(5)	29	66
1992	4	29	67
1993	4	28	68
1994	4	27	70
1995	3	27	70
1996	2	28	70
1997	4	23	73
1998	3	21	76
1999	(5)	21	74

Unweighted base 1991 = 414; 1992 = 819; 1993 = 1249; 1994 = 1690; 1995 = 2103; 1996 = 1689; 1997 = 1284; 1998 = 854; 1999 = 413.

poverty categories reflecting the severity and persistence of poverty experienced by children:

- **no poverty** – not in poverty in any of the five years
- **short-term poverty only** – fewer than three years in poverty and no years in severe poverty
- **short-term and severe poverty** – fewer than three years in poverty but at least one year in severe poverty
- **persistent poverty only** – three or more years in poverty but no years in severe poverty
- **persistent and severe poverty** – three or more years in poverty and at least one year in severe poverty.

These categories differ from the definition of persistent poverty used by the government, described in Section 8.2.1. This is inevitable given that this analysis uses five years of data (whereas the government uses four) and, in addition, these categories also take into account severe poverty, which the government definition does not (see Section 8.2.2). However, as with the government definition of persistent poverty, persistence here is based on the number of years in poverty – ie, at least three out of five – rather than the number of consecutive years in poverty – ie, three or more years in a row.

To some extent these categories are, inevitably, arbitrary. It could be argued, for example, that a more restrictive definition of persistence should be used, so that persistent poverty would be defined as spending four of the five years in poverty, rather than 'just' three. A number of alternative categorisations were tried. Our rationale for the choice adopted was that the categories should not produce artificially large numbers of children in persistent and severe poverty (by, for example, counting more than one year in poverty out of the five as 'persistent poverty') while at the same time providing sufficiently large sample sizes for most of the analyses that we wished to undertake.[2]

A half of children experienced no poverty during the five-year period (50 per cent) (Table 9.2). Of those who were in poverty at some point, the largest proportion experienced persistent poverty only; in other words they had experienced at least three years in poverty but no years in severe

Table 9.2 The experience of poverty over a five-year period

Column per cent

	Percentage of children	Unweighted number of children
No poverty	50	1101
Short-term poverty only	18	386
Short-term and severe poverty	4	76
Persistent poverty only	20	358
Persistent and severe poverty	9	182

Unweighted base = 2103 children

poverty (20 per cent). This was a slightly larger proportion than those who experienced short-term poverty only; that is, fewer than three years in poverty and no experience of severe poverty (18 per cent). Only a small proportion of children had a short-term experience of poverty that included at least one year of severe poverty (short-term and severe poverty: 4 per cent). Almost one in ten children experienced poverty that was both persistent and severe during the five-year period (9 per cent).

The level of persistent poverty, with or without experiences of severe poverty (29 per cent), appears to be larger than that found using the 'official' measure, reported in Section 8.2.1. This is, however, to be expected since this analysis has defined persistent poverty as at least three out of five years in poverty, rather than three out of four years in poverty, as in the official measure. Nevertheless, it should be of concern that over a five-year period nearly one in ten children experienced at least three years of poverty, of which at least one was severe. In particular, it should be borne in mind that the severe income poverty line is lower than Income Support levels (see Section 8.4.1).

It is worth re-emphasising that this analysis measures only a five-year period of childhood; therefore some of these children will have experienced poverty before the five year period in which they were studied and/or go on to experience poverty after the period. Only when the length of time over which it is possible to study childhood expands will it be possible to estimate the persistence of poverty over the whole of childhood.

9.3 Transitions between severe, non-severe and no poverty

Implicit in the poverty categorisation described above is the notion of movement between severe, non-severe and no poverty. However, these categories, while providing a useful broad description of children's experiences of poverty, do not tell us how often these transitions took place, or how likely it was that children moved to or from each poverty status. These dynamics can provide useful insights into the experience of poverty, a number of which are briefly discussed in this section.[3]

A child had a greater than one in eight chance of experiencing severe poverty during the five years of their childhood over which they were analysed; 13 per cent of children were in severe poverty for at least one out of the five years. This compares with 48 per cent of children experiencing non-severe poverty for at least one year, and 88 per cent of children who experienced a year or more of no poverty. This last result means that 12 per cent of children were in poverty, severe or non-severe, for all five years. (See Annex I for details regarding the number of years children spent in severe, non-severe and no poverty.)

9.3.1 Number of spells in severe, non-severe and no poverty

A very large majority of children who experienced severe poverty during the five-year period had just one period, or 'spell' (as such periods are referred to by analysts), of severe poverty (91 per cent), ie, if they left severe poverty, they did not return to severe poverty again within the five-year phase of childhood (Figure 9.1). A large majority of children who had a spell not in poverty also only experienced one period of such a status (84 per cent). On the other hand, children who experienced a completed[4] spell of non-severe poverty were likely to return to it for a further spell of non-severe poverty in a later year (29 per cent had at least a second spell). Below we investigate the length of spells in each of the poverty states and which poverty state children moved from and to. However, what is important to note here is that if children left non-severe poverty they were more likely to return to it

than was the case for leaving and returning to severe poverty and no poverty.

9.3.2 Length of time spent in severe, non-severe and no poverty

Although experiencing one spell in severe poverty or one spell not in poverty was more likely than experiencing one spell of non-severe poverty, for children who experienced severe poverty this one spell was very likely to last for just one year, whereas one spell of no poverty was much more likely to last for all five years (Figure 9.2).

Eighty-six per cent of children in their first spell of severe poverty remained there for just one year, 10 per cent for two years and the remaining 4 per cent for longer than two years. In one sense it is perhaps comforting that the prevalence of longer-term severe poverty spells was relatively small. However, the implications for the life experiences of the 3 per cent of children who, over five years of their lives, lived in severe poverty on a minimum of two occasions, are likely to be serious. It should be recalled that these children were living in households with less than 27 per cent of median income and below the Income Support level.

By contrast, just 45 per cent of first spells in non-severe poverty lasted for only one year and, while 18 per cent lasted for only two years, 17 per cent lasted for all five years. Later chapters investigate whether more persistent, if less severe poverty implies a worse condition than less persistent, more severe poverty by comparing, for example, experiences of financial difficulties, debt, ownership of consumer durables and problems

Figure 9.1 Number of spells in severe, non-severe and no poverty

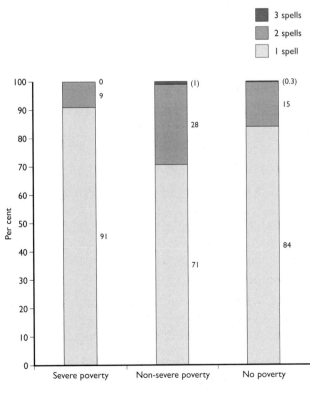

Unweighted base = 2103 children

with the home for children in the poverty persistence and severity categories described above.

Not being in poverty (no poverty) was the most stable of states. Fifty-six per cent of children in their first spell not in poverty remained there for all five years. However, 18 per cent of children in their first spell not in poverty went into poverty (either severe or not) after one year.

9.3.3 Destinations of children leaving severe, non-severe and no poverty

When children left severe, non-severe and no poverty, where did they move to? The majority of children who left severe poverty, moved only as far as non-severe poverty (Figure 9.3). Seventy-two per cent of spells in severe poverty were followed by a spell in non-severe poverty, with the remaining 28 per cent moving to the no poverty state.

Figure 9.2 Length of time children spent in severe, non-severe and no poverty during their first spell in each

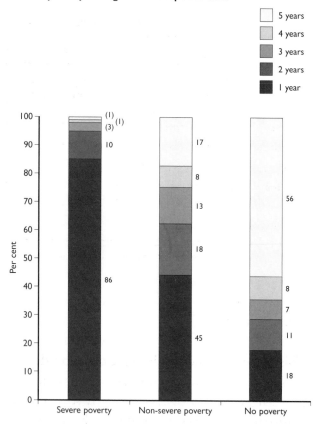

Unweighted base – severe poverty first spell = 258 children, non-severe poverty first spell = 952 children, no poverty first spell = 1887 children

Figure 9.3 Destinations of children leaving severe, non-severe or no poverty before the final year

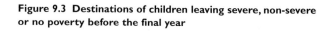
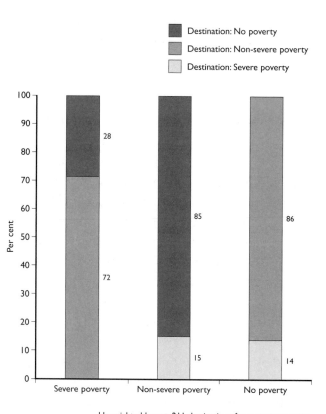

Unweighted base = 211 destinations from severe poverty, 745 destinations from non-severe poverty, 613 destinations from no poverty

The likelihood of a move out of poverty from non-severe poverty was much greater: 85 per cent of spells in non-severe poverty were followed by a spell of no poverty, whereas 15 per cent moved from non-severe to severe poverty. Interestingly, 14 per cent of moves from no poverty were also to severe poverty, which suggests that there was approximately the same chance of entering severe poverty from higher income (no poverty) households as there was from lower income (non-severe poverty) households.[5] Of course, it is possible that children moving from no poverty to severe poverty in consecutive years had spent a period of months in non-severe poverty (which would not have been captured in the data) before moving to severe poverty.[6] However, it remains the case that their chances of moving to severe poverty one year later were not greatly different from those moving to severe poverty from non-severe poverty.

Whether children who experience a sharper drop in family income fare worse than those who experience a smaller drop is open to debate. Children in higher income families may have assets (savings and other resources) to fall back on to smooth the transition, which those moving from non-severe poverty may not have. However, if such assets are low or non-existent, the adjustment to such a severe loss of income could be much greater than an adjustment from an already constrained income.

Another way of examining the data involves summing all moves from one poverty state to another (Table 9.3). This simplistic approach loses some detail but shows more clearly where the main changes occurred. Forty-one per cent of

all moves were from non-severe to no poverty, while the opposite occurred in just 34 per cent of moves. Nine per cent of moves were from non-severe poverty to severe poverty, while 7 per cent transferred in the other direction. Finally, while 5 per cent of moves occurred from no poverty to severe poverty, 4 per cent moved from severe poverty to no poverty. These results imply that, while the non-severe poverty rate should be decreasing (as, indeed, was suggested at the beginning of this chapter in Table 9.1), the severe poverty rate should be remaining approximately equal (again as shown in Table 9.1).

Table 9.3 Proportion of all movements occurring between severe, non-severe and no poverty

Column per cent

Poverty transition	Proportion of all movements
Non-severe poverty to no poverty	41
No poverty to non-severe poverty	34
Severe poverty to non-severe poverty	9
Non-severe poverty to severe poverty	7
Severe poverty to no poverty	4
No poverty to severe poverty	5

Unweighted base = 1569 movements between poverty states

9.4 Summary

This section has focused in some detail on the transitions between severe, non-severe and no poverty that underlie the five poverty severity and persistence categories. It has shown that around one in eight children experienced severe poverty at some stage of the five years over which they were followed; that is, they were in households with very low incomes of less than 27 per cent of the median.[7] However, this experience did not usually last until the following year, and very few children returned to severe poverty once they had moved out of it. For the majority, the route out of severe poverty was only as far as non-severe poverty rather than a move out of poverty. In contrast, routes into severe poverty were about as likely to be sudden and straight from no poverty, as they were to be gradual via non-severe poverty. The result of these transitions was that nearly one in ten children experienced poverty that was persistent **and** involved at least one year of severity (ie, persistent and severe poverty).

Given that periods spent in severe poverty were mainly very short, did children who had experienced severe poverty differ in terms of their characteristics or 'exclusion experiences' from children who had not experienced severe poverty, or was the persistence of poverty, rather than its severity, more important? These questions are explored in the following chapters.

10 Characteristics of children in persistent and severe poverty

This chapter examines the characteristics of children in each of the poverty severity and persistence categories to see which factors in children's lives were most likely to be associated with persistent and severe poverty. The regression analysis in Part 1 of this report showed that severe poverty at a point in time was strongly associated with:

- living in a household with no workers
- living in local authority accommodation
- being in a household in receipt of Income Support or Jobseeker's Allowance
- living in the South or Midlands of England
- having parents with no educational qualifications.

Clearly, just as income (and, therefore, experiences of poverty) can change from year to year, so too can some of the children's characteristics. A child's lone parent may re-partner so that the child moves from being in a one parent family to being in a two parent family; unemployed parents may find work; a new baby may be born; a child's family may move to a different region of the country, and so forth.

It is possible that some of these changes in socio-demographic characteristics might act as **triggers for changes** in poverty status, although it is also possible that changes in some characteristics may be **consequences of changes** in poverty status. As a result, we cannot say conclusively, for example, that changes in characteristics cause severe poverty – it may be that severe poverty causes a change in characteristics. However, knowledge of the association of some of these socio-demographic characteristics with the poverty categories can help

to illuminate some of the processes underlying poverty transitions.

Changes in socio-demographic characteristics have been conceptualised in two ways. First, the number of years in which a child experienced a particular characteristic is measured (for example, the number of years with no workers in the household). Secondly, characteristics are considered in terms of the **transitions** that occurred over the five years (for example, the transition between having workers and no workers in the household). In addition, the analysis considers the relationship between the five poverty categories and:

- characteristics that will not, or are very unlikely to, change over time (ethnicity of the household and the parent's educational qualifications)
- characteristics that change in the same way and at the same rate for all children (age of the child)
- characteristics more easily summarised as an average over the five years (age of the youngest child).

The analysis presented in this chapter is exploratory, relying on simple comparisons of the percentages in each poverty category according to experiences of change. This procedure is undertaken separately for each of the socio-demographic characteristics, while more sophisticated modelling attempts to identify the more influential factors relating to experiences of persistent and severe poverty. This analysis is a first step on the path to illuminating our understanding of how changes in personal circumstances relate to the length and/or the depth of childhood poverty. A next step would be to identify the changes between different circumstances and estimate the likelihood of entering different poverty states when these changes happen. However, this more complex procedure is beyond the scope of this study, largely because of the small sample size.

Section 10.1 describes the characteristics (number of years and transitions) of children and their families separately. Section 10.2 considers all the characteristics together to see which characteristics independently best predict whether a child would be in persistent and severe poverty.

10.1 Characteristics of children in persistent and severe poverty

10.1.1 Employment status of adults in the household

This section considers the relationship between the current employment status of adults in a child's household – in other words, their employment status in the week before each annual interview – and the child's poverty status. The analysis focuses on children in households with no, one, or two or more workers.[1]

NUMBER OF YEARS WITHOUT WORKERS
Two-thirds of all children had at least one household member in employment in each of the five years (66 per cent) and the vast majority of children who experienced no poverty had a worker in the household throughout the period (94 per cent) (Table 10.1). This contrasts starkly

with children who had experienced some form of poverty. In general, the worse the poverty state, the longer children had spent with no workers in the household, so that almost two-fifths of children in persistent and severe poverty and in persistent poverty only had spent either four years or all years with no workers (38 and 37 per cent respectively). Children in the remaining two short-term poverty states were far less likely to have spent lengthy periods without workers; only 5 per cent or less of these children had been without workers in the household for four or five years.

However, perhaps the most interesting finding in Table 10.1 is the relatively large proportion of children who had experienced some degree of poverty and who were in a household where at least one adult worked in each of the five years. A quarter of children in persistent poverty only, and one in six children in persistent and severe poverty had spent none of the five years without a worker in the household (25 and 17 per cent respectively). It seems that, in addition to work not ensuring that children will avoid poverty at a point in time, even continuous[2] work is no guarantee that a child will avoid poverty that is persistent and/or severe.

Nevertheless, it remains clear that the chances of a child avoiding poverty in general, and particularly the worst forms of poverty over time, were improved if they lived in households with continuous work. But to what extent is childhood poverty associated with changes in the employment status of households? In other words, were children who lived with adults who moved

Table 10.1 Number of years with no workers in household by poverty status

Column per cent

	Persistent and severe poverty	Persistent poverty only	Short-term and severe poverty	Short-term poverty only	No poverty	All children
Always no workers	19	22	(2)	(2)	(1)	7
4 years no workers	19	15	(3)	(2)	(<0.5)	5
3 years no workers	15	15	(3)	(4)	(1)	5
2 years no workers	15	15	(12)	12	(1)	7
1 year no workers	16	9	45	18	4	10
No years no workers	17	25	35	62	94	66

Unweighted base = 2092 children

frequently between work and no work at greater risk of (severe and persistent) poverty than those who lived throughout the five years in a workless household?

TRANSITIONS BETWEEN NO WORKERS, ONE WORKER, AND TWO OR MORE WORKERS IN THE HOUSEHOLD

Examining the transitions that children's households made in the number of workers is revealing (Table 10.2). While always having two or more workers in the household almost always protected children from persistent and/or severe poverty, always having one worker did not necessarily do so: between 7 per cent and 9 per cent of children who had experienced some degree of poverty had lived throughout the five-year period with one worker. Again, it seems that continuous work does not necessarily protect children from (persistent and/or severe) poverty.

In terms of the transitions children experienced between having no, one, and two or more workers

in the household, it is clear that **experiencing** a household employment transition did not appear to be particularly damaging in terms of poverty status, rather it was the **type** of transition that made an impact. Moving between having two or more workers and one worker did not seem to be associated with severe or persistent poverty (it was, however, associated with no poverty and short-term poverty only). But moving between having one worker and no worker was associated with very high levels of severe and/or persistent poverty, higher even than among children who lived with no workers in each year. Almost a half of children who experienced persistent and severe poverty had made a transition between having one worker and no worker in the household (49 per cent), while a fifth lived with no workers in each year (19 per cent). More than a third of those in persistent poverty only (36 per cent) had made a similar transition, while over a fifth lived with no workers in each year (22 per cent). Looked at from the opposite end of the scale, around two-fifths of children in no poverty had

Table 10.2 Transition between no, one or two or more worker household by poverty status

Column per cent

	Persistent and severe poverty	Persistent poverty only	Short-term and severe poverty	Short-term poverty only	No poverty	All children
Always 2+ workers	(1)	(1)	(3)	13	44	25
Always 1 worker	(7)	9	(8)	9	11	10
Transitions between 2+ and 1 workers	9	14	(24)	41	40	32
Transitions between 2+ and no workers	(3)	8	(17)	9	(1)	5
Transitions between 2+, 1 and no workers	12	10	24	12	(2)	7
Transitions between 1 and no workers	49	36	(23)	14	(2)	16
Always no workers	19	22	(2)	(2)	(1)	7

Unweighted base = 2092 children

either had two or more workers in the household each year (44 per cent) or had made the transition between having two or more and one worker (40 per cent).

It could be, of course, that the number of these transitions was important; that is, the more transitions between work and no work, the worse the risk of persistent and/or severe poverty. Further analysis of the number of transitions experienced by children showed that this was not the case (figures not shown). The **number** of transitions did not greatly change the proportions in each poverty status it was the **type** of transition that mattered. In other words, any movement between work and no work was associated with severe and/or persistent poverty, particularly for those who experienced the change from one worker to no worker in the household.

In addition, the **order** of transitions was analysed to try to determine whether a move from no work to work appeared to be more or less advantageous in terms of poverty status than a move in the opposite direction. It would be assumed that moving from no work to work would, in most cases, be advantageous in terms of income. However, at the time of this analysis, those moving into work could be affected by low and/or part-time wages (the majority of these data were collected before the introduction of the minimum wage and Working Families Tax Credit) and/or a loss of other benefits, which could decrease rather than increase the household income.

For all children, experiencing a transition from work to no work was as likely as a transition from no work to work (7 per cent and 8 per cent respectively) (Table 10.3). However, children in persistent poverty only appear to have been twice as likely to have been in a household that moved from no work to work than vice versa (20 and 10 per cent respectively). For children in persistent and severe poverty, on the other hand, a transition from work to no work was slightly more likely than vice versa (20 compared to 16 per cent). The most likely transition for both these poverty states, however, was two or more transitions between work and no work (23 and 29 per cent respectively). Indeed, all children who experienced some degree of poverty were much more likely than children in no poverty (3 per cent) to have experienced two or more transitions between work and no work, but this was particularly the case for children in short-term and severe poverty (41 per cent).

10.1.2 Main source of income

Having considered the employment patterns within children's households, it seems sensible to explore the source from which the household received most of its income in each year over the five-year period. The BHPS collects detailed information on annual household income from work, benefit, pension, transfer (that is, income gained from a transfer of income from one household to another) and investment incomes. From these annual figures (measured from September to August), it was possible to identify which of these five sources was the main source of income for the household during the year. So, unlike household employment status which was measured at the time of interview, main source of income was calculated for the whole year.

Table 10.3 Order of transitions between no, one or two or more worker household by poverty status

Column per cent

	Persistent and severe poverty	Persistent poverty only	Short-term and severe poverty	Short-term poverty only	No poverty	All children
Always 2+ workers	(1)	(1)	(3)	13	44	25
Always 1 worker	(7)	9	(8)	9	11	10
Transitions between 2+ and 1 workers	9	14	(24)	41	40	32
1 transition – work to no work	20	10	(20)	10	(1)	7
1 transition – no work to work	16	20	(3)	8	(1)	8
2+ transitions between work and no work*	29	23	41	18	3	13
Always no workers	19	22	(2)	(2)	(1)	7

Unweighted base = 2092 children

*This will, by definition, include those who moved from work to no work and vice versa

(work to no work to work; no work to work to no work)

NUMBER OF YEARS INCOME FROM WORK WAS MAIN SOURCE OF INCOME

First, it is clear that living in a household in which income from work was the main annual source of income throughout the five-year period provided children by far the best, if not complete, protection from poverty (Table 10.4). More than nine in ten children who experienced no poverty during the five-year period were in households where work was the main source of income throughout (93 per cent), compared with less than one in ten children in persistent and severe poverty (9 per cent). The worse the poverty status, the greater the proportion of households which had spent longer periods without work as the main income source. Almost a quarter of children in persistent and severe poverty had spent no years in households with work as the main source of income (23 per cent), but interestingly an even greater proportion, over two-fifths, of those in persistent poverty only had done so (42 per cent). Even when the main source of income was from

work for three out of the five years, this affected large proportions of children in the worst poverty states: 19 per cent in persistent and severe poverty and 11 per cent in persistent poverty only.

However, again, it should be noted that even having continuous income from work did not necessarily protect children from poverty, with between 9 per cent (persistent and severe poverty) and 59 per cent (short-term poverty only) of children having lived in households with work as the main source of income in all years.

TRANSITIONS BETWEEN MAIN SOURCE OF INCOME

While it is apparent that, broadly, income from work gives children the best protection from poverty, it is important to understand what happens when households make the transition from one main source of income to another. To what extent did policies in place between

Table 10.4 Number of years with work as the main source of household income by poverty status

Column per cent

	Persistent and severe poverty	Persistent poverty only	Short-term and severe poverty	Short-term poverty only	No poverty	All children
All years	(9)	17	44	59	93	62
4 years	12	(4)	27	15	4	7
3 years	19	11	(16)	14	(1)	7
2 years	17	15	(5)	(3)	(1)	6
1 year	20	13	(5)	(4)	(<0.5)	5
No years	23	42	(3)	7	(1)	12

Unweighted base = 2088 children

1991 and 1999 cushion movements between income from work to income from benefits, and vice versa? For the purposes of this analysis, work income has been combined with pension, transfer and investment income ('other' income), as numbers receiving the latter three sources were small and, in general, their poverty rates were much more similar to those of households with work rather than benefits as their main source of income. So this section investigates transitions between work/other income and benefit income.

Living in a household that made transitions between income from work to income from benefits and vice versa was associated with higher rates of persistent and severe poverty for children than being in a household whose main income was benefits throughout the five-year period (Table 10.5). Among children in persistent and severe poverty, almost three in ten households had made two or more transitions between benefit and income from work (28 per cent), compared

with a fifth whose main source of income had been benefits throughout the period (21 per cent). This number of transitions was greater than for children in persistent poverty only, among whom 40 per cent had benefits as their main source of household income in all years, and only 13 per cent had made two or more transitions. However, among children in short-term and severe poverty the proportion who had experienced two or more transitions (29 per cent) was as high as among those in persistent and severe poverty. Therefore, it seems that repeated transitions between work and benefit income was associated with short spells of severe poverty, as well as longer spells of poverty that were both persistent and severe. In addition, it seems that even one transition from work to benefit income **or** from benefit to work income could be problematic, both accounting for a fifth of children in persistent and severe poverty (20 per cent in each case).

Table 10.5 Transitions between income from work/other and from benefits by poverty status

Column per cent

	Persistent and severe poverty	Persistent poverty only	Short-term and severe poverty	Short-term poverty only	No poverty	All children
Always work/'other' income	11	17	60	69	97	67
Always benefit income	21	40	0	(6)	(1)	12
Transition from work/'other' to benefit income	20	13	(8)	6	(1)	6
Transition from benefit to work/ 'other' income	20	17	(3)	12	(1)	8
2+ transitions between benefit and work/'other' income	28	13	(29)	8	(1)	8

Unweighted base = 2088 children

10.1.3 Receipt of Income Support, Unemployment Benefit or Jobseeker's Allowance

The BHPS asks respondents which benefits they had received during the year. For this analysis, respondents' answers have been combined to indicate whether anyone in the household had received at least one of the main out-of-work benefits during the years in question – that is, whether anyone in the household had received Income Support (IS) and/or Unemployment Benefit (UB) prior to 1996, or Income Support and/or Jobseeker's Allowance (JSA) from 1996 onwards.[3] From these data it is possible to determine the number of years children lived in households in which someone was in receipt of one or more of these benefits and whether any transitions between the years occurred. In what follows, receipt of benefits should be taken to mean receipt of one or more of these benefits.

NUMBER OF YEARS IN RECEIPT OF IS, UB OR JSA

Children who experienced no poverty were very likely to live in a household that had not received the main out-of-work benefits at any point during the five years (79 per cent), compared with only 14 per cent of children in persistent and severe poverty (Table 10.6). Conversely, children who were in persistent poverty (with or without severity) were the most likely to have received benefits in all years. Those in persistent poverty only had done so to a greater extent than those in persistent and severe poverty (41 per cent and 29 per cent respectively), compared with only 1 per cent of those who had experienced no poverty. Again, in general, the longer the period spent in receipt of benefits the higher the proportions of children accounted for in each

poverty state. The exception to this is the 19 per cent of children in persistent and severe poverty who had received benefits for three out of the five years. This is probably explained by their more regular transitions between no worker and one worker, as seen in Section 10.1.1.

However, not receiving benefits did not necessarily protect a child from poverty. Between 14 per cent (persistent and severe poverty) and 68 per cent (short-term and severe poverty) of children who had experienced some degree of poverty had not been in receipt of benefits at any point during the five years. Some of these children's families may have been entitled to benefits that they did not take-up. However, other families may not have been entitled to these benefits, for example, because their levels of savings were too high or they were students (as seems likely for children in short-term and severe poverty, see Section 10.1.4).

TRANSITIONS BETWEEN RECEIVING AND NOT RECEIVING IS, UB OR JSA

As Table 10.6 revealed, any poverty increased the chances of having received benefits at some point. However, transitions between receipt and no receipt of benefits had important associations with poverty of any degree. Children who had experienced poverty were approximately one and a half times more likely to have experienced two or more benefit transitions than a child who had experienced no poverty.

Looking in more detail at the order of transitions, it becomes clear that, while children in short-term poverty (with or without a period of severe poverty) or persistent poverty only, were twice

Table 10.6 Number of years in receipt of IS, UB or JSA by poverty status

Column per cent

	Persistent and severe poverty	Persistent poverty only	Short-term and severe poverty	Short-term poverty only	No poverty	All children
All years	29	41	(2)	9	(1)	13
4 years	17	14	(3)	5	(1)	6
3 years	19	12	(4)	9	2	7
2 years	12	10	(4)	9	5	7
1 year	(10)	6	(19)	17	12	12
No years	14	17	68	52	79	56

Unweighted base = 2103 children

Table 10.7 Transitions between receiving and not receiving IS, UB or JSA by poverty status

Column per cent

	Persistent and severe poverty	Persistent poverty only	Short-term and severe poverty	Short-term poverty only	No poverty	All children
Receiving all years	29	41	(2)	9	(1)	13
Receiving no years	14	17	68	52	79	56
No receipt to receipt	18	10	(9)	10	5	8
Receipt to no receipt	23	18	(7)	14	7	12
Two or more transitions	16	14	(15)	15	9	12

Unweighted base = 2103 children

as likely as children in no poverty to live in households that had moved from no receipt to receipt of benefits, children in persistent and severe poverty were almost three times as likely to have done so (Table 10.7). However, transitions from receipt to no receipt were more likely to have occurred for children in persistent poverty, with or without severity, than for other children.

This quite complicated picture of the relationship between benefit receipt and poverty has produced a comparatively simple message: that transitions between receiving and not receiving benefit have important consequences for experiences of persistent and severe poverty in childhood. While persistent poverty only appeared more strongly related to consistent benefit receipt, experiences of persistent and severe poverty had strong associations with transitions between receipt and no receipt.

10.1.4 Family type

It is possible for changes to occur in the type of family in which a child lives. Lone parents will re-partner so that their children move from being in a lone parent family to a couple family; some couples will separate so that their children move into a lone parent family. Research evidence has found that 28 per cent of families with children were lone parent families in 2001 and that, by 2001, 11 per cent of low-income couples in 1999 had become lone parents and 15 per cent of lone parents in 1999 had become couples (Marsh and Perry, 2003). In addition, because the cohorts being studied in this analysis include children up to the age of 19 years, it is also possible for some children to have left home and begun to live independently. Therefore, for the purposes of this analysis children could be living with two, one or no parents in each of the five years.

NUMBER OF YEARS LIVING IN A LONE PARENT FAMILY

Among children who experienced no poverty in the five-year period, the vast majority had spent all five years in a couple household (85 per cent) and less than one in ten had been in a lone parent household throughout the period (9 per cent) (Table 10.8).

It appears that being in a lone parent family for fewer than five years (but more than none) was more strongly associated with persistent and severe poverty or short-term poverty (with or without an experience of severe poverty) than living in a lone parent family throughout the period. Approximately three in ten children in persistent and severe poverty had lived in a lone parent family for between one and four years (29 per cent), compared with a quarter who had lived with a lone parent for the whole five years (24 per cent). This was not the case, however, for children in persistent poverty only, among whom fewer than a fifth had lived with a lone parent for between one and four years (18 per cent), but two-fifths for all five years (42 per cent). This suggests that it may have been the **transition** between living in a lone parent and couple family (or vice versa) that was related

Table 10.8 Number of years in each family type by poverty status

Column per cent

	Persistent and severe poverty	Persistent poverty only	Short-term and severe poverty	Short-term poverty only	No poverty	All children
Always couple	47	39	49	55	85	66
Always lone parent	24	42	(9)	19	9	19
1–2 years lone parent	(12)	7	(8)	9	2	6
3–4 years lone parent	17	11	(11)	11	(2)	7
No years lone parent, but not always couple*	(1)	(1)	(24)	6	2	3

Unweighted base = 2100 children

*In other words, moved from living in a couple household to living independently.

Table 10.9 Transitions between family type by poverty status

Column per cent

	Persistent and severe poverty	Persistent poverty only	Short-term and severe poverty	Short-term poverty only	No poverty	All children
Always couple	47	39	49	55	85	66
Always lone parent	24	42	(9)	19	9	19
Couple to lone parent	17	14	(15)	10	3	8
Lone parent to couple	(3)	(2)	0	(4)	(<0.5)	(1)
Couple to independent	(1)	(1)	(24)	6	(2)	3
Lone parent to independent	(4)	(1)	(2)	(5)	(1)	2
2 or more transitions	(5)	(1)	(2)	(1)	(<0.5)	(1)

Unweighted base = 2098 children

to **severe** poverty status, rather than a long continuous period in a lone parent family which was more likely to be associated with **persistent** poverty.

TRANSITIONS BETWEEN LIVING IN A COUPLE, LONE PARENT OR INDEPENDENT HOUSEHOLD

A large majority of children remained in the same family type in all five years (85 per cent) so that 15 per cent made at least one transition in their family type over the five years (Table 10.9). Eight per cent moved from a couple to a lone parent household, while 1 per cent experienced the reverse. Five per cent of children moved to independent living, 3 per cent from a couple household and 2 per cent from a lone parent household. The remaining 1 per cent of children experienced more than one family type transition over the five years.

Although numbers of children who experienced a transition of family type are small, the results

suggest that a transition from a couple to a lone parent household (and vice versa) was more likely to have occurred for children in poverty, severe and/or persistent poverty in particular. Transitions to independence were much more likely to have taken place amongst children in short-term and severe poverty, suggesting that leaving the parental home may be related to a short-term, dramatic, drop of income, perhaps whilst studying away from home.

10.1.5 Age of child and number of children in the family

The age of the child is not a characteristic that can be analysed dynamically since all children age at the same rate. The cohort style of this analysis means that children were analysed as they aged from 0 to 4 years, 5 to 9 years, 10 to 14 years or 15 to 19 years. Comparing children in these groups shows that, in general, younger children were over-represented in the groups that experienced the worst poverty, and older children

Table 10.10 Age of child by poverty status

Column per cent

	Persistent and severe poverty	Persistent poverty only	Short-term and severe poverty	Short-term poverty only	No poverty	All children
0–4 years	38	32	40	24	29	30
5–9 years	30	33	(12)	28	22	26
10–14 years	22	24	(12)	21	25	24
15–19 years	(10)	12	36	27	24	21

Unweighted base = 2103 children

were under-represented. Children in the youngest age group were over-represented, in particular, in persistent and severe poverty and short-term and severe poverty (38 and 40 per cent respectively) (Table 10.10).

Another way of looking at the effect of family composition on poverty is to take into account the age of the youngest child in the family (Table 10.11). The average age of the youngest child in the household was calculated over the five years and grouped as above. This shows more clearly the disproportionately serious effect of poverty on children when there were young children present in the household. Sixty-five per cent of children in persistent and severe poverty were in a household with a child in the youngest age group, and only 3 per cent with a child in the oldest age group. The same pattern, if less stark, can be seen among children in persistent poverty only and in short-term and severe poverty, and is in contrast to the pattern for children in no poverty, among whom 39 per cent had a youngest child with an average age of between 0 and 4 years and 15 per cent between 15 and 19 years.

Table 10.11 Average age of youngest child in the family over five years by poverty status

Column per cent

	Persistent and severe poverty	Persistent poverty only	Short-term and severe poverty	Short-term poverty only	No poverty	All children
0–4 years	65	56	46	39	39	45
5–9 years	21	24	(16)	23	23	23
10–14 years	11	17	(10)	23	22	20
15–19 years	(3)	(3)	(28)	16	15	12

Unweighted base = 2103 children

The average number of children in the household over the five years was calculated and it was found that family size was also associated with poverty status. The larger the average number of children in the household during the five-year period, the greater the chances of children experiencing persistent poverty, with or without severity (Table 10.12). Among children who were in persistent and severe poverty, only one in 10 were in a one child family (11 per cent), whereas almost three-fifths were in families with an average of three or more children (59 per cent). A similar pattern can be seen among children in persistent poverty only.

Both contrast with children in no poverty, among whom a quarter were in a one child family (26 per cent) and a further quarter in families with three or more children (24 per cent).

Changes in the number of children in a household over a five-year period also seemed to be associated with an increased risk of poverty (Table 10.13). This was particularly the case where a new child, or children, joined the household, or where the household experienced children both joining and leaving the household. Almost three in ten children in persistent and

Table 10.12 Average number of children in the household over five years by poverty status

Column per cent

	Persistent and severe poverty	Persistent poverty only	Short-term and severe poverty	Short-term poverty only	No poverty	All children
One	(11)	15	(25)	19	26	21
Two	30	35	49	43	50	44
Three or more	59	50	27	39	24	36

Unweighted base = 2103 children

Table 10.13 Changes in the number of children in the household by poverty status

Column per cent

	Persistent and severe poverty	Persistent poverty only	Short-term and severe poverty	Short-term poverty only	No poverty	All children
Same number in all years	58	58	53	60	70	64
Decrease in number	(8)	13	25	19	13	14
Increase in number	28	24	(16)	16	15	18
Both increase and decrease	(7)	6	(6)	5	2	4

Unweighted base = 2103 children

severe poverty (28 per cent), and a quarter of children in persistent poverty only (24 per cent) had experienced new children joining the household, either because of a birth or, possibly, stepchildren being added to the pre-existing family, compared with only one in seven children in no poverty (15 per cent). Although numbers are small, it seems that children in households where children both left and joined the household were almost three times as likely to have experienced some degree of poverty than were children who experienced no poverty. The explanation seems to be that children who experienced both increases and decreases in the number of children in the household were also much more likely to have undergone changes in family type than children in general, particularly a movement to independent living (figures not shown). As Section 10.1.4 has shown, such transitions were particularly likely to be associated with poverty.

10.1.6 Ethnicity of adults in the household

The ethnicity of adult household members in 1995 was used to determine whether a child's household contained all white adults or at least one adult of non-white ethnicity.

It seems that living in a household where at least one adult was of non-white ethnicity not only increased the risk of poverty, but the poverty experienced was more likely to be persistent, with or without severity (Table 10.14). Children in persistent and severe poverty and in persistent poverty only (both 10 per cent) were more than twice as likely to have been in 'non-white' households than children in no poverty (4 per cent).

10.1.7 Parents' highest educational qualifications

The highest educational qualifications of a child's parent(s) were measured in the first year that a child joined their cohort. The poverty experienced by children whose parents had no educational qualifications was far more likely to be persistent, with or without severity, than by children whose parents did have qualifications (Table 10.15). More than a fifth of children who were in persistent and severe poverty (21 per cent), and almost a third of children in persistent poverty only (32 per cent), had parents with no educational qualifications, compared with only one in fourteen children who experienced no poverty (7 per cent). At the other extreme, only

Table 10.14 Ethnicity of adults in the household by poverty status

Column per cent

	Persistent and severe poverty	Persistent poverty only	Short-term and severe poverty	Short-term poverty only	No poverty	All children
All adults white	90	90	97	97	96	95
At least one adult of non-white ethnicity	(10)	10	(3)	(4)	4	6

Unweighted base = 2098 children

Table 10.15 Parental educational qualifications by poverty status

Column per cent

	Persistent and severe poverty	Persistent poverty only	Short-term and severe poverty	Short-term poverty only	No poverty	All children
Higher than A level or equivalent	(10)	(4)	40	20	34	24
A levels or equivalent	21	15	31	22	27	23
O levels/CSE or equivalent	47	50	(22)	42	32	38
None of these	21	32	(7)	16	7	15

Unweighted base = 2092 children

one in ten children in persistent and severe poverty (10 per cent), and one in 25 in persistent poverty only (4 per cent), had parents with qualifications above A Level standard, compared with more than a third of children who experienced no poverty (34 per cent).

10.1.8 Living with an adult with a limiting illness in the household

In this section the interaction between living with an adult with a limiting illness and the poverty status of children is explored, first by the length of time that a child was in these circumstances and, secondly, by any changes that took place in the health status of adults during the five-year period. To measure experiences of ill health, adult respondents were asked whether or not their health limited their daily activities.[4]

NUMBER OF YEARS LIVING WITH AN ILL ADULT
There was a strong relationship between childhood poverty and living in a household with at least one adult with an illness which limited their daily activities and, in general, the longer a child lived in these circumstances, the worse their poverty experience (Table 10.16). More

than half of children in persistent poverty, with or without an experience of severe poverty, had lived with an ill adult for at least one year during the five-year period (both 56 per cent). This compared with only just over a quarter of children who had experienced no poverty (26 per cent). Approximately one in ten children in persistent poverty had spent the entire five-year period living with an ill adult; 10 per cent of those in persistent and severe poverty and 8 per cent of those in persistent poverty only, compared with only 3 per cent of children who experienced no poverty.

It seems that children who lived throughout the period with an ill adult were somewhat better off than those who had lived with an ill adult for three or four years. The former group were 'only' three times more likely to be in persistent poverty (with or without severity) than to have experienced no poverty, whereas children who had lived with an ill adult for three or four years were approximately five times more likely to be in persistent poverty than in no poverty. The reason for this is unclear, but is possibly related to the benefits system which may have provided more

financial security through Invalidity Benefit/
Incapacity Benefit to those who were permanently
sick or disabled than to those who moved in and
out of illness. This is explored further below.

TRANSITIONS BETWEEN LIVING WITH AN ILL ADULT AND NOT

The evidence seems to confirm that the benefits
system better protected children living with an
ill adult if they were in that state for long periods
of time, since the number of transitions that

children experienced between living with an ill
adult and no ill adult was associated with severe
and persistent poverty and persistent poverty only
(Table 10.17). More than a fifth of children in
persistent and severe poverty (21 per cent), and
over a quarter of those in persistent poverty only
(26 per cent), had experienced two or more
transitions between living with an ill adult and
not during the five-year period. This compared
with one in ten children in persistent and severe
poverty (10 per cent), and one in 13 of those in

Table 10.16 Number of years living with an ill adult by poverty status

Column per cent

	Persistent and severe poverty	Persistent poverty only	Short-term and severe poverty	Short-term poverty only	No poverty	All children
All years	(10)	8	(6)	(4)	3	5
3–4 years	21	19	(8)	11	4	10
1–2 years	25	30	(19)	27	18	23
No years	44	44	67	59	74	62

Unweighted base = 2103 children

Table 10.17 Transitions between living with an ill adult and not by poverty status

Column per cent

	Persistent and severe poverty	Persistent poverty only	Short-term and severe poverty	Short-term poverty only	No poverty	All children
No years with ill adult	44	44	67	59	74	62
Always at least one ill adult	(10)	8	(6)	(4)	3	5
No ill adults to ill adults	14	14	(6)	12	7	10
Ill adults to no ill adults	(11)	9	(9)	7	4	6
Two or more transitions	21	26	(12)	18	12	17

Unweighted base = 2103 children

persistent poverty only (8 per cent), who had always lived with an ill adult. It seems, therefore, that whilst living with an ill adult was associated with higher risks of experiencing poverty, and particularly poverty that was persistent and/or severe, living with adults who had periods of sickness interspersed with periods of good health was at least as disadvantageous.

10.1.9 Housing tenure

NUMBER OF YEARS LIVING IN RENTED ACCOMMODATION

The longer a child lived in rented accommodation the worse their poverty experience was likely to be (Table 10.18). Over four-fifths of children who experienced no poverty (83 per cent) had lived in owner-occupied accommodation throughout, compared with just over a fifth of children in persistent poverty only (22 per cent), and over a quarter of those in persistent and severe poverty (28 per cent). Even renting for a short period seemed to be associated with poverty: around two-fifths of children who had experienced short-term and severe poverty (39 per cent), and over

one in ten children in short-term poverty only (12 per cent), had lived in rented accommodation for only one or two of the five years.

For children in the two worst poverty states, by contrast, the association seems to have been with always having lived in rented accommodation, rather than moving from one accommodation type to another. More than three-fifths of children in persistent and severe poverty had lived in rented accommodation for the whole five years (62 per cent), and more than seven in ten of children in persistent poverty only (71 per cent).

TRANSITIONS BETWEEN OWNING AND RENTING ACCOMMODATION

The above finding is borne out by an examination of the number of transitions that children made between rented and owner-occupied accommodation during the five-year period (Table 10.19, overleaf). It seems clear that moving from owner-occupied to rented accommodation was associated with an increased risk of experiencing short-term and severe poverty; 26 per cent of children in this poverty group had moved from

Table 10.18 Number of years in rented accommodation by poverty status

Column per cent

	Persistent and severe poverty	Persistent poverty only	Short-term and severe poverty	Short-term poverty only	No poverty	All children
Always rent	62	71	(11)	30	8	29
3–4 years renting	(7)	(5)	(3)	8	3	4
1–2 years renting	(3)	(3)	39	12	6	8
Always own	28	22	47	51	83	59

Unweighted base = 2084 children

Table 10.19 Transitions in housing tenure by poverty status

Column per cent

	Persistent and severe poverty	Persistent poverty only	Short-term and severe poverty	Short-term poverty only	No poverty	All children
Always own	28	22	48	51	83	59
Always rent	62	71	(11)	30	8	29
Own to rent	(7)	(5)	(26)	11	4	6
Rent to own	(3)	(3)	(8)	7	5	4
Two or more transitions	(1)	(<0.5)	(8)	(2)	(1)	1

Unweighted base = 2084 children

owning to renting, compared with only 7 per cent in persistent and severe poverty. Logically, of course, this short-term and severe poverty is likely to become persistent and severe poverty as the length of time spent in rented accommodation increases. It seems that the longer a child lived in rented accommodation the greater the risk of poverty and, particularly, persistent and/or severe poverty. However, it should be noted that children in short-term and severe poverty were also the most likely to have moved to independent living (see Table 10.9), suggesting that this poverty may not become persistent, but rather that these young people were in a short-term situation as they began their independent living, perhaps as students.

10.1.10 Country and region

Although small numbers in the analysis make it impossible to explore in any detail the circumstances of children in the different regions or countries of Britain, it is worth examining the poverty status of children, first by the country/region they lived in for the majority of the five years (Table 10.20), and, secondly,

comparing the circumstances of those who moved country/region during the five-year period with those who did not move (Table 10.21).

Children who lived in the Midlands for most of the five-year period were over-represented in the worst poverty groups (although it should be noted that the numbers of children surveyed in Scotland and Wales were small, so it is difficult to draw conclusions regarding these countries – see Table 10.20). Almost a third of children in persistent and severe poverty (32 per cent), and in persistent poverty only (30 per cent), lived in the Midlands, compared with only a fifth of children who experienced no poverty (19 per cent). However, living in other areas of Britain was associated with other types of poverty, with almost half of children in short-term and severe poverty living in the South of England (46 per cent).

Movements between countries or regions did not seem to be associated with an increased risk of poverty, in that children who moved were no more likely to be in three of the poverty groups

Table 10.20 Country or region lived in for majority of years by poverty status

Column per cent

	Persistent and severe poverty	Persistent poverty only	Short-term and severe poverty	Short-term poverty only	No poverty	All children
London	(11)	13	(13)	10	9	11
South	17	19	46	36	31	29
Midlands	32	30	(15)	22	19	23
North	28	23	(21)	21	29	26
Wales	(6)	6	(2)	5	4	5
Scotland	(6)	10	(4)	7	8	8

Unweighted base = 2102 children

Table 10.21 Regional transitions by poverty status

Column per cent

	Persistent and severe poverty	Persistent poverty only	Short-term and severe poverty	Short-term poverty only	No poverty	All children
Always London	(8)	12	(12)	9	9	10
Always South	17	17	32	32	29	26
Always Midlands	31	30	(12)	20	18	22
Always North	26	21	(16)	19	28	25
Always Wales	(5)	6	(1)	5	4	4
Always Scotland	(6)	10	(4)	7	8	8
Moved region	(6)	(4)	(23)	7	5	6

Unweighted base = 2102 children

than in the no poverty group (Table 10.21). The exception was the group of children in short-term and severe poverty, among whom 23 per cent had moved region, compared with only 5 per cent of children in no poverty. It seems likely that this can be explained to some degree by the much greater proportion of children in short-term and severe poverty who moved away from their parents, possibly as students.

10.2 Explaining persistent and severe poverty

The associations presented in Section 10.1 provide a useful description of how the different poverty categories relate to each of a number of socio-demographic factors. However, many of these socio-demographic factors are themselves inter-related and so we need to explore the extent to which each factor was independently related to poverty, over and above any relationship that factor had with poverty through its inter-relationships with other factors. For example, while it is clear that living in rented accommodation was related to poverty, is this relationship still important once receipt of benefits in these households is taken into account? In order to achieve this, a 'multinomial regression analysis' was used, with each of the characteristics of children in no poverty being compared with the characteristics of those who were in short-term poverty only, persistent poverty only and persistent and severe poverty.[5, 6]

Table 10.22 contains only results from the analysis that reached statistical significance. In other words, there is only, at most, a 5 per cent possibility that these results have occurred by chance. The symbol '+' means that the characteristic was positively associated with a child being in the poverty category (it increased the risk of poverty), while the symbol '–' means that it was negatively associated (it decreased the risk of poverty). Annex J provides more details about the model, showing the odds ratios for each characteristic (that is, the number of times more or less likely children in each poverty category were to have each significant characteristic).

In summary, Table 10.22 shows that children who experienced **any form of poverty** were different from children who experienced no poverty in a number of ways. Children experiencing poverty of any type were **more** likely to have:
- been in a no worker household for one year
- lived in rented accommodation for five years

- had adults in the household who were ill for between three and four years
- lived in the Midlands
- received benefits for three or four years and
- lived in a household with an average of three or more children.

In addition, they were all **less** likely to have had parents educated to degree level than children in no poverty.

The fact that these characteristics were significant, even for children who were in short-term poverty only, suggests that there was something distinctly different about children, and families, who had ever experienced poverty. This clearly has a number of important policy consequences for the reduction of child poverty, discussed in Chapter 15.

10.2.1 Comparing children in persistent and severe poverty with those in no poverty

The results of the model suggest that the characteristics important in predicting a period of **persistent and severe poverty**, as distinct from no poverty (in addition to those described above), included:
- to have been without workers in all years (at the time of interview)
- to have received benefits for between two and five years
- to have had one year without workers and
- to have had two or more transitions between the main source of income.

It would appear that there were at least two distinct groups of children in persistent and severe poverty as defined by the work and benefit characteristics of their households. The first group was made up of those whose financial situation appeared relatively stable, albeit bleak. These were children living in workless households for all five years of the childhood phase over which they were observed.[7] In comparison to children in households with workers for all five years, children in workless households were more likely to face persistent and severe poverty. If they had spent five years in receipt of benefits, the odds of persistent and severe poverty were also greater. As many of those children in workless households would have also spent all five years dependent on benefits as a main income source, their actual risk of persistent and severe poverty was very much greater than that of children living in households with workers for all five years and who received no benefits, as the chances[8] (shown in Annex J) of experiencing each of the characteristics are multiplicative.

However, although spending all five years in a workless household appears to be a powerful driving force behind persistent and severe poverty, reference back to Table 10.1 shows that only 19 per cent of children who experienced persistent and severe poverty spent all five years in a workless household. Therefore, over four-fifths of children in persistent and severe poverty did not face all five years in a workless household – other characteristics must have been at the root of their poverty experiences.

The second group of children, defined by the work and benefit characteristics of their households, is those who experienced income volatility, ie, two or more income transitions between work/other income and benefit income as the main source of household income. Twenty-eight per cent of children in persistent and severe poverty experienced this circumstance (Table 10.5). Children whose households underwent two or more such transitions were much more likely to be in persistent and severe poverty than children who did not experience these transitions (Table 10.22). As these children in households which experienced multiple main source of income changes must also have spent at least one year in receipt of benefits, it is likely that their actual chances of persistent and severe poverty were compounded further. The risk of persistent and severe poverty would also be further compounded if the household had spent one year without a worker.

Persistent and severe poverty was **negatively** related to spending five years in a lone parent family, which is not to say that children in lone parent families were absent from persistent and severe poverty. Rather, once their other circumstances were taken into account, children in stable lone parent families were less likely to face persistent and severe poverty than children who constantly lived in a couple family.

Clearly, not all of persistent and severe poverty was related to being in a workless household for five years, or experiencing two or more transitions in main income source. Other characteristics in the model that were independently associated with an increased risk of persistent and severe poverty included having three or more children in the household, a youngest child in the household aged 0–4 years, and living in the Midlands.

10.2.2 Comparing children in persistent and severe poverty with those in persistent poverty only

Understanding the processes that are associated with severe poverty among children in persistent poverty is important if policy interventions are to try and avoid children moving into severe poverty. To address this issue, a comparison is made between the characteristics that distinguished children in persistent poverty only from children in persistent and severe poverty (comparing the second and third columns of Table 10.22).

This comparison shows the particular importance of transitions for the experience of persistent and severe poverty. The characteristics associated with **lowered** chances of children experiencing persistent and severe poverty rather than persistent poverty only were:

- having been in a lone parent family for five years
- never having had work as a main source of annual income (measured in the year prior to the interview)
- having moved between no worker and two workers (or vice versa).

Conversely, characteristics associated with **increased** chances were:

- having had no workers in all years (measured at the time of interview)
- having had two or more transitions in their main source of income
- having an average of three or more children in the household and
- having parents educated to A level or degree level.

There is an apparent paradox evident in the results shown in Section 10.1 and those of Section 10.2. Section 10.1 found that approximately a fifth of children in persistent poverty only and persistent and severe poverty had no workers in each of the five years (Table 10.3). Yet, in this section, not having workers for five years is a significant factor for predicting persistent and severe poverty, but not for predicting persistent poverty only. Why then should worklessness distinguish these two groups?[9]

It appears that for children in both these poverty states, time spent in a workless household relates also to time spent with benefit as a main source of income, as would be expected. However, while 22 per cent of children in persistent poverty only were in workless households, a much higher proportion (40 per cent) spent all five years with benefit as their main income source (Table 10.5). In comparison, for children in persistent and severe poverty the children who spent all five years in a workless household (19 per cent), typically were also those whose main income source for all five years was benefits (21 per cent). Therefore, it appears that, for children in persistent poverty only, the group whose main income source was benefits for all five years included not only some whose parents were non-workers, but also some whose parents were working but at insufficient levels or for insufficient periods during the year for earnings to be their main income source. In contrast, among children in persistent and severe poverty, children whose parents worked did so to such an extent that earnings were sufficient to make apparent transitions in main income sources, ie, their earnings were great enough to mean that they could leave benefits and earnings became the greater source of income during the year (either through earning greater amounts or by working for longer periods during the year); the consequences of such transitions were influential, as shown in the model.

It is interesting to note that children experiencing persistent and severe poverty were more likely to have parents educated to A level or higher than parents of children in persistent poverty only, suggesting that high levels of education did not always prevent periods of very low income.

However, it may explain why some of these families were able to gain (higher paid) work, as suggested above. In addition, children living in larger families (with three or more dependent children) were more likely to experience persistent and severe poverty, rather than persistent poverty only. It is also clear that while long periods spent in a lone parent family were associated with an increased risk of persistent poverty only, this was not associated with persistent and severe poverty.

Table 10.22 Significant characteristics explaining poverty persistence and severity

	Short-term poverty only	Persistent poverty only	Persistent and severe poverty
Number of years without workers			
5			+
2	+		
1	+	+	+
Employment transitions			
2 or more and 1 worker	+		
Number of years in lone parent family			
5			–
3–4	+		
Number of years in rented accommodation			
5	+	+	+
Number of years with ill adult(s) in household			
3–4	+	+	+
1–2	+	+	
Transitions between ill and no ill adult in household			
2+ transitions		+	

continued overleaf

Table 10.22 Significant characteristics explaining poverty persistence and severity *continued*

	Short-term poverty only	Persistent poverty only	Persistent and severe poverty
Number of years work main source of income			
0		+	
1		+	
Main source of income transitions			
2+ transitions			+
Number of years in receipt of benefits			
5	+		+
4	+	+	+
3	+	+	+
2			+
1	+		
Region lived in most years			
Midlands	+	+	+
Average number of children in household			
3 or more	+	+	+
2	+		+
Age of child			
5–9 years	+		
Highest parental educational qualification			
Degree or higher	–	–	–
A level or equivalent	–	–	
Average age of youngest child in household			
0–4 years		+	+
5– 9 years		+	
10–14 years		+	

Unweighted base = 1659 children

Note: All odds have a significance of at least 95 per cent.

11 Persistent and severe poverty in childhood and household exclusion

Part 1 of this report showed that severe poverty can be closely associated with experiences of social exclusion. The following chapters consider the relationship between poverty persistence and severity on the one hand and experiences of social exclusion by households (this chapter), parents (Chapter 12) and children (Chapter 13) on the other.

This chapter describes the experiences of household exclusion from which, by definition, parents will not be able to protect their children. Children are part of the household and, therefore, will experience these 'exclusions' to the same degree as other household members. These experiences are compared for children in each of the poverty states.

Four dimensions of exclusion are considered:
- financial difficulties that children's households experienced in terms of problems in meeting the costs of accommodation and other household utilities
- whether children's households owned particular consumer durables, focusing on those most likely to be used by children: a colour television, a video recorder and a home computer
- whether children's households went without specific 'necessities' because they could not be afforded
- reported problems with accommodation and the local area.

Some questions are asked in the BHPS in only a limited number of years. Questions about meeting the costs of accommodation and consumer durables are asked in all years of the survey and, therefore, information is available for all five years of the child cohorts. The years for which the other measures have been analysed are described in each relevant section below.

11.1 Household financial difficulties

As previous research by the authors has suggested, a child in an income poor household will not necessarily experience adverse effects directly if parents are able to maintain the child's consumption by sacrificing their own needs (Middleton and Adelman, 2003). However, if income is so low as to lead to other financial difficulties, such as problems paying for accommodation, a cutback on other living expenses, going into debt or falling behind with payments, then children will inevitably experience the consequences.

The household questionnaire of the BHPS asks a number of questions related to difficulties in paying for accommodation – first, simply whether there had been difficulties and, for those who had experienced difficulties, whether these had resulted in borrowing or cutbacks, and/or meant that they were two or more months late with their housing payments.

11.1.1 Difficulties paying for accommodation
Over two-thirds of children lived in households which had no difficulties in paying for their accommodation in any of the five years (69 per cent) (Table 11.1). It is striking that there were few differences between children who experienced the different types of poverty on this measure of exclusion.

However, the difference between children experiencing any degree of poverty and those children never experiencing poverty was very great. Less than three-fifths of children who had experienced some degree of poverty were in households that had not experienced housing payment difficulties (52 to 60 per cent), compared with four-fifths of children who had experienced no poverty (80 per cent). In addition, while just 5 per cent of children who experienced no poverty were in households experiencing difficulties for three or more years, children in persistent poverty only and children in short-term poverty only were at least twice as likely to have done so (11 per cent and 10 per cent respectively). Children in persistent and severe poverty were almost three times as likely (14 per cent).

Further analysis suggests that experiencing difficulties in paying for housing was related, once again, to transitions. The children who were more likely to live in households experiencing at least one year of difficulties were those who had changed family type, had moved from having workers to no workers (and vice versa) and had experienced transitions in receipt of IS/JSA (figures not shown). The results of Sections 10.1 and 10.2 suggest that the reasons families not experiencing these transitions were also less likely to experience difficulties paying for their accommodation were that they were never in poverty (ie, always in a couple family, always with a worker in the household, never in receipt of benefit), or they were likely to be protected from such difficulties through consistent receipt of Housing Benefit (ie, always a lone parent family, always with no worker, always in receipt of benefit). Qualitative research would be required to understand why such difficulties were being experienced by those making transitions.

Households that had experienced difficulties paying for their accommodation were then asked whether this had resulted in them borrowing money, being two or more months late with their housing payments or experiencing cutbacks in order to pay for accommodation. In the following analyses, in the years in which these questions were not asked (because households reported no

Table 11.1 **Number of years household has had difficulties paying for accommodation by poverty status**

Column per cent

	Persistent and severe poverty	Persistent poverty only	Short-term and severe poverty	Short-term poverty only	No poverty	All children
Always no difficulties	52	60	58	58	80	69
1 year	20	17	(19)	21	12	16
2 years	14	12	(18)	11	4	8
3 or more years	14	11	(5)	10	5	8

Unweighted base = 1929 children

difficulties paying for their accommodation), these households were recorded as not experiencing these associated problems.

11.1.2 Housing payment difficulties required borrowing

Over nine-tenths of children were in households that did not borrow money to cover housing payments in any of the five years (92 per cent) (Table 11.2). The proportion of children in households that borrowed money to cover housing payments in at least one of the years rose as poverty became more severe and/or persistent. So that, while just 5 per cent of children in no poverty were in households that borrowed money in at least one year, this was the case for 15 per cent of children in persistent and severe poverty.

11.1.3 Late housing payments

One in ten children lived in households which had been two or more months late with their housing payments in at least one year (10 per cent) (Table 11.3). The poverty status of children living in households which had been behind with payments in at least one year follows the same pattern as seen above; the greater the poverty persistence and/or severity, the more likely they were to be in households with late payments. Again, just 5 per cent of children in no poverty had such experiences, while children in short-term poverty, with or without severity, were twice as likely to have done so (both 11 per cent), children in persistent poverty only were three times as likely (16 per cent), and children in persistent and severe poverty almost four times more likely (19 per cent).

Table 11.2 Housing payment difficulties required borrowing by poverty status

Column per cent

	Persistent and severe poverty	Persistent poverty only	Short-term and severe poverty	Short-term poverty only	No poverty	All children
Always no borrowing	85	89	88	91	95	92
1 or more years of borrowing	15	11	(13)	9	5	8

Unweighted base = 1925 children

Table 11.3 Housing payments late by two or more months by poverty status

Column per cent

	Persistent and severe poverty	Persistent poverty only	Short-term and severe poverty	Short-term poverty only	No poverty	All children
Never been late	81	84	89	89	95	90
1 or more years been late	19	16	(11)	11	5	10

Unweighted base = 1961 children

11.1.4 Housing payments required cutbacks

Over a quarter of all children lived in households that had cut back in order to pay for their accommodation in at least one year (28 per cent), a much larger proportion than had been required to borrow money or had been late with housing payments. Once again, there were differences according to the child's poverty status, with children in persistent and severe poverty the worst off. Approximately a half of these children lived in households that had cut back in at least one year (47 per cent), and for one eighth cutbacks had occurred in three or more years (13 per cent). Children in persistent poverty only and short-term poverty only appeared to have experienced

cutbacks to almost the same extent as one another.

The experiences of children who experienced any degree of poverty contrast starkly to the experiences of children in no poverty, among whom less than a sixth were in households that experienced cutbacks in at least one year (16 per cent), and only one in 25 for three or more years (4 per cent).

11.1.5 Problems paying household bills

In Wave 5 of the BHPS only, households were asked whether in the last 12 months they had been unable to pay for utilities such as gas,

Table 11.4 Number of years housing payments required cutbacks by poverty status

Column per cent

	Persistent and severe poverty	Persistent poverty only	Short-term and severe poverty	Short-term poverty only	No poverty	All children
Always no cutbacks	53	63	56	63	84	72
1 year	22	18	(23)	21	9	15
2 years	13	10	(21)	10	3	8
3 or more years	13	8	0	(6)	4	6

Unweighted base = 1954 children

Table 11.5 Unable to pay household bills in the last 12 months by poverty status (1995 only)

Column per cent

	Persistent and severe poverty	Persistent poverty only	Short-term and severe poverty	Short-term poverty only	No poverty	All children
Able to pay bills	68	71	89	81	93	84
Unable to pay bills	32	29	(11)	19	7	16

Unweighted base = 2083 children

electricity, and water in the time allowed. All children in our sample were in the survey in 1995 and, therefore, all children were included in this analysis. However, it should be remembered that this is the household's experience for just one year and will not necessarily mean that the same situation would have existed in all the years for which the child's poverty status was measured.

In 1995, 16 per cent of children lived in households that were unable to pay their household bills in the time allowed (Table 11.5). Again, there were marked differences between children's experiences depending on their poverty status. Just one in fourteen children in no poverty had such an experience (7 per cent), compared to approximately a third of children in persistent poverty, with or without an experience of severe poverty, 32 per cent of children in persistent and severe poverty, and 29 per cent of children in persistent poverty only.

11.2 Consumer durables

The findings of qualitative research have shown clearly the importance which parents place on children's ability to participate fully in the social sphere (Middleton et al., 1994). This will include having experiences within the home that can then be shared with children's friends and peers outside the home. Therefore, the household's ownership of three consumer durables, each of which might be considered particularly important in ensuring that children have the same or similar experiences to their peers, has been analysed according to the child's poverty status.

11.2.1 Colour television

In the PSE, 56 per cent of adults said that they believed that a television was a necessity that everyone in Britain should be able to afford and 98 per cent of PSE respondents owned a colour television (Table 11.6).

Only a small minority (5 per cent) of all children did not have a colour television in their household in all five years, and only 1 per cent of children who had experienced no poverty. In contrast, 12 per cent of children in persistent poverty, whether or not they had experienced severe poverty, lived in households that did not have a colour television in at least one year.

11.2.2 Video recorder

In the PSE, a video recorder was regarded as a necessity by only 19 per cent of adults and,

Table 11.6 Colour television in the household by poverty status

Column per cent

	Persistent and severe poverty	Persistent poverty only	Short-term and severe poverty	Short-term poverty only	No poverty	All children
Always had colour television	88	88	89	95	99	95
1 or more years without	12	12	(11)	(5)	(1)	5

Unweighted base = 2101 children

Table 11.7 Video recorder in the household by poverty status

Column per cent

	Persistent and severe poverty	Persistent poverty only	Short-term and severe poverty	Short-term poverty only	No poverty	All children
Always had video	63	71	70	79	92	82
I year without video	17	16	27	15	5	11
2 or more years without video	20	14	(3)	(6)	3	7

Unweighted base = 2101 children

therefore, it was not included in the list of adult items in the deprivation measure. Nevertheless, 91 per cent of PSE respondents actually owned a video recorder.

As expected, the proportion of children who did not have a video recorder in their household was much higher than for lacking a colour television (Table 11.7). Eighteen per cent of children did not have access to a video recorder in all five years but, again, experiences differed according to children's poverty status. Just 8 per cent of children in no poverty went without a video for at least one year, a much lower proportion than even for children experiencing short-term poverty only (21 per cent). Children in persistent and severe poverty were as likely as those in persistent poverty only to lack a video for one year (17 and 16 per cent respectively), but were more likely to have gone without for two or more years (20 and 14 per cent respectively).

11.2.3 Home computer
Although only 11 per cent of adults in the PSE survey thought a home computer was a necessity, 43 per cent of respondents owned one.

The rapidly growing penetration of home computers and the increased use of computers in schools suggests that children without such facilities at home are likely to be increasingly disadvantaged. This is also shown by the fact that the proportion of *parents* regarding a 'computer suitable for schoolwork' as a necessity grew considerably over just four years in the 1990s, from 20 per cent in 1995 to 38 per cent in 1999 (Gordon et al., 2000).

Just under a quarter of all children had a home computer in the household for all five years (23 per cent) (Table 11.8). Twenty-seven per cent did not have one in any year, while approximately one in eight did not have a computer for one, two, three or four years (12 and 13 per cent). As with colour televisions and video recorders, children who experienced no poverty were the most likely to have had access to a home computer in all years (33 per cent). They were more than twice as likely to have had a computer than children in short-term poverty only (15 per cent), and more than three times as likely as children in persistent poverty, with or without an experience of severe poverty (10 per cent).

However, children in short-term poverty, with or without an experience of severe poverty, were as likely as children in no poverty to have gone without a home computer in all years (20 per cent in each case). Another difference to the other consumer durables is that, in this case, children in persistent poverty only were more likely than children in persistent and severe poverty to not have had access to a home computer in any year (almost a half compared to two-fifths respectively). This lower level of 'permanent exclusion' occurred because a much larger proportion of children in persistent and severe poverty had a computer for two years than was the case for children in persistent poverty only (17 compared to 6 per cent respectively). This seems to suggest that the former of these households were more likely to have bought a home computer in the years in which they were not in poverty.

11.3 'Necessities' would like but cannot afford

Part 1 of this report provided a wealth of information about the relationship of necessities deprivation to income poverty and social exclusion. The BHPS household questionnaire asked households similar questions to those in the PSE about whether they went without six items/activities because they could not be afforded. This means that some analysis can be undertaken to compare the circumstances of children in persistent and/or severe poverty with regard to their access to necessities (see Annex K for a comparison of the questions). Unfortunately, however, these questions were only asked from 1996 onwards, so that the analysis had to exclude those children entering the sample in 1991 as no values for these questions were available. This analysis has selected the final year that children were in the sample in order to examine the effect of five years of severe and/or persistent poverty on the affordability of necessities.

Table 11.8 Home computer in the household by poverty status

Column per cent

	Persistent and severe poverty	Persistent poverty only	Short-term and severe poverty	Short-term poverty only	No poverty	All children
Always had home computer	(10)	10	28	15	33	23
1 year without home computer	(6)	5	(19)	16	14	12
2 years without home computer	17	6	(19)	14	13	12
3 years without home computer	15	14	(6)	14	11	12
4 years without home computer	14	19	(9)	20	9	13
5 years without home computer	39	47	(20)	20	20	27

Unweighted base = 2101 children

Children's households were most likely to be unable to afford an annual holiday (27 per cent) and least likely to be unable to afford to keep their home adequately warm (2 per cent) (Figure 11.1). Once again, there were stark differences between children who had experienced no poverty and children who had experienced poverty, especially those whose poverty was persistent, with or without severity. Of these latter children, over a half lived in households that were unable to afford an annual holiday, approximately three in ten in households that could not afford to replace worn out furniture, and a fifth could not afford to have friends or family round for a drink or meal once a month. Children in persistent poverty only were more likely to live in a household that had gone without meat, chicken or fish every second day than children in persistent and severe poverty (12 compared to 6 per cent). It is unclear why there should be such a difference on only this

measure. However, what is clear is that persistent poverty (with or without severity) had a greater detrimental effect on the provision of necessities than short-term poverty. This suggests that the measure of poverty in Part 1 of this report is likely to be associated with persistent poverty.

11.4 Problems with accommodation and local area

The BHPS includes questions about specific problems households have with their accommodation and with their local area, many of which are similar to the measures included in the PSE and analysed in Part 1 of this report. However, these measures were not included in the BHPS until 1996 which means that children entering the survey in 1991 could not be included in this analysis. For the remaining children, the

Figure 11.1 'Necessities' would like but cannot afford by poverty status

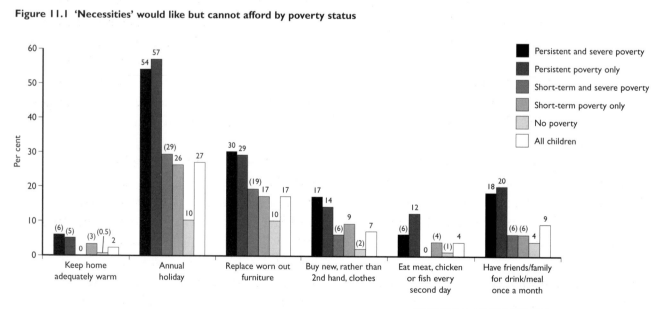

Unweighted base = 1664–1685 children
(differences due to missing values)

Figure 11.2 Problems with accommodation by poverty status

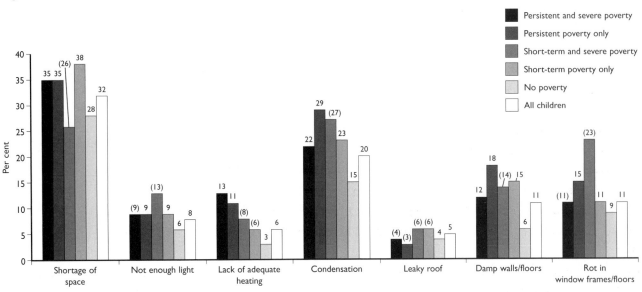

Unweighted base = 1683–1687 children
(differences due to missing values)

analysis considers the problems experienced by households in the final year that children were in their cohort, so as to identify housing and area problems at the end of their possible time spent in persistent and/or severe poverty.

11.4.1 Problems with accommodation

Differences in the proportions of children experiencing accommodation problems were generally small between children who experienced some degree of poverty, although children in short-term and severe poverty were slightly more likely than other children in poverty to experience rot in window frames and floors, and to not have enough light (Figure 11.2).

However, children who had experienced poverty to any degree were much more likely to experience each of the problems than children

who had experienced no poverty. Particularly striking were the much higher proportions of children in poverty who lacked adequate heating and who lived in homes with damp in the walls or floors. These findings are similar to those that emerged from Part 1 which also found few differences between severely and non-severely poor children, but great differences between poor children and non-poor children.

11.4.2 Problems with the local area

The BHPS includes questions about four local area problems, each of which was also included in the PSE. As was the case for housing problems, differences between children who experienced some degree of poverty were generally small, although children in short-term and severe poverty were slightly worse off, being the most likely to experience street noise and vandalism

Figure 11.3 Problems with the local area by poverty status

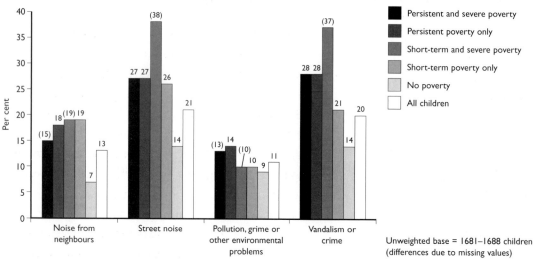

Unweighted base = 1681–1688 children
(differences due to missing values)

and crime (Figure 11.3). This is in contrast to the analysis in Part 1 which found large differences between children in severe and non-severe poverty and that, in general, problems with the local area were much greater among children experiencing severe poverty.

However, as in Part 1, differences between poor children and non-poor children were

large. Children who had experienced any degree of poverty were approximately twice as likely as children who had experienced no poverty to live in households that reported three out of the four problems, the exception being the experience of pollution, grime or other environmental problems for which there was little difference between all groups.

12 Persistent and severe poverty in childhood and exclusion among parents

The previous chapter investigated the relationship between exclusion at the household level and children's poverty status. However, parents themselves may experience other dimensions of exclusion which may, in turn, affect the lives of their children to some extent. A description of the relationship between some of these experiences and children's poverty status is the subject of this chapter.

Four dimensions of exclusion are considered:
- parents' satisfaction with the area in which they live and with their home
- the extent of parents' 'civic engagement'
- parents' personal experiences of savings and debt
- parents' emotional well-being.

In order to ensure that the measures reflect the experiences of the child's parent(s), rather than just any adult who happened to be in the household, the responses of the child's mother have been analysed for children living with their mother or, if the child's mother was not in the household, the father's responses have been used. In the small number of cases where children were living independently, the child's own responses have been analysed. As with the measures of household exclusion, measures in this chapter were not asked in every year of the BHPS. If the measure was not available in all years, the relevant section makes clear for which years the analysis was carried out.

12.1 Parents' satisfaction with local area and home

Part 1 of this report found that severely poor children were much more likely to live in areas with which their parents were dissatisfied and in which there were a number of specific problems than was the case for children in non-severe poverty and, to a greater extent, for children in no poverty. However, in contrast, the previous chapter has suggested fewer differences between severely and non-severely poor children's experiences of local area problems. This section focuses on two specific questions that were asked of parents which reflect their satisfaction with their neighbourhood and their home: whether they liked their neighbourhood and whether they would prefer to move house.

12.1.1 Satisfaction with present neighbourhood
Three-quarters of children had parents who liked their neighbourhood in all five years (Table 12.1). Just over one in ten had parents who liked their neighbourhood in four out of the five years (11 per cent). Parents of the remaining one in seven children had only liked their neighbourhood for three or less years (14 per cent).

Children who had experienced no poverty were the most likely to have parents who had been satisfied with their neighbourhood in every year (84 per cent). This figure compares starkly to children in persistent poverty, with or without severity, of whom just over three-fifths had parents who liked their neighbourhood in all years (62 and 63 per cent respectively).

Children in persistent poverty, with or without severity, were the most likely to have parents who had been satisfied with their neighbourhood for three or fewer years (21 and 20 per cent respectively), compared to only one in ten children who had experienced no poverty (9 per cent). However, children in short-term poverty only also had a high level of parents satisfied with their neighbourhood for three or fewer years (17 per cent).

12.1.2 Prefer to move house

Just under a third of children had parents who had never wanted to move during the five years (30 per cent), and one in six had parents who would have preferred to move in every year (16 per cent) (Table 12.2).

Differences between the five poverty categories based on this measure are small. Children who were in persistent poverty, with or without severity, and short-term poverty only, appear to have been slightly more likely to have had parents who wished to move in at least one year than those in no poverty, or in short-term and severe poverty.

Table 12.1 Parents liking of present neighbourhood by child's poverty status

Column per cent

	Persistent and severe poverty	Persistent poverty only	Short-term and severe poverty	Short-term poverty only	No poverty	All children
Always liked neighbourhood	62	63	76	70	84	75
4 years liked neighbourhood	17	17	(15)	13	7	11
3 or fewer years liked neighbourhood	21	20	(9)	17	9	14

Unweighted base = 2017 children

Table 12.2 Parents preferring to move house by poverty status

Column per cent

	Persistent and severe poverty	Persistent poverty only	Short-term and severe poverty	Short-term poverty only	No poverty	All children
Always prefer to stay in house	26	23	37	25	34	30
1 year prefer to move	13	16	(18)	16	19	17
2 years prefer to move	19	15	(11)	16	12	14
3 years prefer to move	15	14	(6)	11	11	12
4 years prefer to move	(13)	17	(19)	14	9	12
5 years prefer to move	15	15	(10)	18	16	16

Unweighted base = 1996 children

In each year that parents said that they wished to move, they were asked to give their main reason for wanting to move from a choice of 25 reasons. This large choice meant that the numbers in the analysis were too small to produce any robust findings with the exception that, in all poverty states, the main reason parents wished to move was to gain larger accommodation. In the first year of the cohorts this ranged from being the main reason for 17 per cent of children in persistent poverty (with or without severity), to 31 per cent of children in short-term and severe poverty and no poverty. This is to be expected, given the large proportion who reported that there was a shortage of space in their home (Section 11.4.1).

12.2 Parents' civic engagement

The British government and, indeed, governments in democratic systems throughout Europe have become increasingly concerned with a decline in what can be called 'civic engagement' or 'civic participation'. The UN Development Programme has defined such participation as occurring when people are 'closely involved in the economic, social, cultural and political processes that affect their lives' (United Nations Development Programme, 1993, p.21). Concern in the UK has focused on the young, particularly on the declining numbers of young people voting in elections, highlighted, for example, by the government's Children and Young People's Unit project 'YVote? YNotVote?' to determine why young people have so little interest in politics (see http://www.cypu.gov.uk/corporate/about/yvote.cfm for details). Previously published

evidence from the PSE has shown that the youngest (16–34 years) and oldest adults (over 65 years) were most likely to be disengaged from civic and/or community activities (Gordon et al. 2000, p.67). Since August 2002 citizenship education has been a compulsory part of the curriculum for 11- to 16-year-olds in English schools. But research in the UK and abroad has suggested that the extent to which children and young people grow up to participate in their communities is likely to depend to some extent on the levels of such engagement among their parents (Egerton, 2002; Stone and Hughes, 2001).

In this section, the relationship between civic (dis)engagement among parents and childhood poverty is examined, first by analysing whether or not parents had voted in the previous general election and, secondly, by exploring their membership of, and activism in, a range of community organisations.

12.2.1 Voting
In Waves 2, 5, 7, 8, and 9 of the BHPS adults were asked whether or not they had voted in the previous general election. Responses have been used from the last election that occurred during the child's presence in the sample. So, for children entering the sample in 1991 and 1992 responses relating to voting in the 1991 election were analysed, and for children entering in 1993, 1994 or 1995, voting in the 1997 election.

Four-fifths of children had parents who said they had voted in the last general election (81 per cent) (Figure 12.1). However, there were variations according to poverty status. Of children who had

Figure 12.1 Parent voted in last general election by child's poverty status

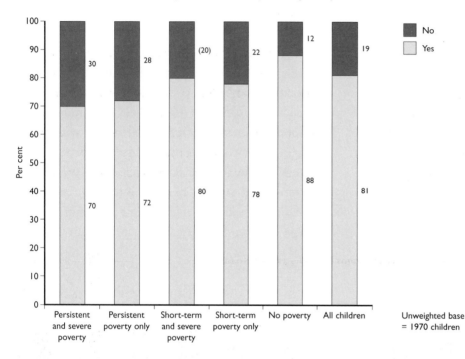

experienced no poverty, almost nine-tenths had parents who had voted (88 per cent), compared to seven-tenths of children in persistent poverty, with or without severity (70 and 72 per cent respectively).

12.2.2 Membership and activity in organisations

Parents were asked whether they were a member of 16 organisations and whether they joined in the activities of these organisations on a regular basis. These included organisations related to work (trade union, professional organisations), community involvement (parents' association, tenants' and residents' association, voluntary service group), social engagement (social group, sports club) and others. However, these questions

were asked only in Waves 1–5, 7, and 9. Therefore, this analysis focuses on parents' responses in the final year of the cohort where possible (for children entering the sample in Waves 1, 3 and 5), and the penultimate year of the cohort otherwise (for children entering the sample in Waves 2 and 4). The number of organisations of which parents were members and in which they were active have been totalled.

Children who had experienced no poverty were much more likely to have parents who were members of, or active in, one or more organisation. Just a third of these children had parents who were not a member of at least one organisation (35 per cent), and two-fifths who were not active in at least one organisation

(42 per cent). These figures are in stark contrast to those for children who had experienced poverty, particularly those in persistent poverty, with or without severity, of whom around two-thirds had parents who were not a member of, or active in, at least one organisation (all between 62 and 67 per cent). These children were around a third as likely to have parents who were members of, or active in, two or more organisations than children in no poverty.

12.3 Parents' experiences of savings and debt

Part 1 showed that children in severe poverty were more likely to live in households that were 'financially excluded' in that they were more likely to be in debt and less likely to have bank accounts. Chapter 11 has already suggested that levels of household financial exclusion were worse for children who were in persistent and/or severe

Figure 12.2 Parents' membership of and activity in organisations by child's poverty status

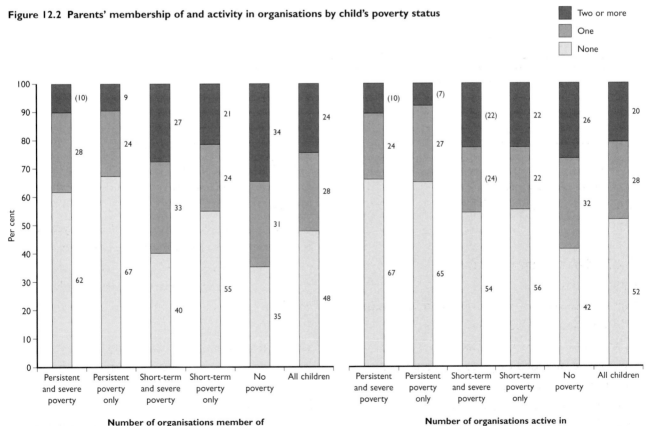

Unweighted base = 2088 children (membership of organisations) and 2078 children (active in organisations)

poverty. In this section parents' personal experiences of savings and debt are examined in relation to children's poverty status.

12.3.1 Savings

Earlier analysis of the PSE has shown that adults in poorer households are particularly unlikely to be able to save 'at least £10 each month for a rainy day or retirement' (Goodwin et al., 2002). However, it is sometimes suggested by economists that households who experience short-term falls in income can 'smooth' their incomes by drawing on savings made in better times. But how is parents' ability to save for their, and their children's, future affected by lengthy periods when their children experience severe and/or persistent poverty?

Almost two-thirds of children had parents who had managed to save at some point during the five-year period (65 per cent), but only one in ten (10 per cent) had saved in all five years (Figure 12.3). However, the impact of poverty on the ability to save is clear, and the worse the experience of poverty the less likely parents were to save. Approximately three-fifths of children in persistent poverty, with or without severity, and approximately a third of children in short-term poverty, with or without severity, had parents who were unable to save in any of the five years. This compares with only one in five children who experienced no poverty whose parents were unable to save in any year. Interestingly, being able to save for one or two of the five years varied only slightly according to poverty status;

Figure 12.3 **Parent's ability to save by child's poverty status**

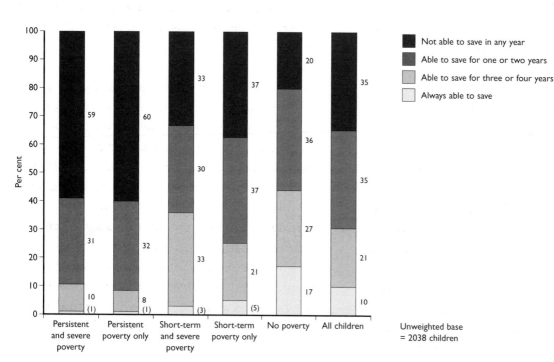

Legend:
- Not able to save in any year
- Able to save for one or two years
- Able to save for three or four years
- Always able to save

Unweighted base = 2038 children

Figure 12.4 Amounts parents saved by child's poverty status[1]

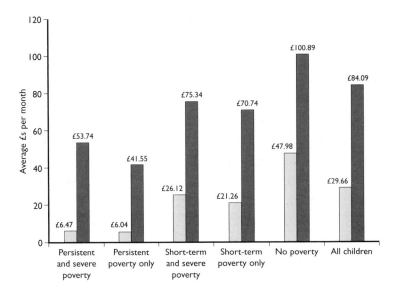

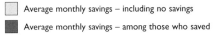

Average monthly savings – including no savings
Average monthly savings – among those who saved

Unweighted base = 1881 (all children) and 1174 (children whose parents saved)

approximately a third of children in all five categories had parents who had managed to save in one or two of the five years, although the definition of the poverty states may mean that such savings took place in the years when the children were not poor.

The extent to which parents are able to cushion their children's poverty will depend not just on whether they are able to save, but on the amount of savings that are made. Figure 12.4 shows parents' average monthly savings over the five-year period, first for all children in each category and, secondly, for only those children who had parents who were able to save in at least one of the years. It is clear that the parents of children who experienced no poverty during the period were able to make far higher levels of average monthly savings than any of the groups of children who experienced poverty. In addition, the parents of

children who had experienced persistent and severe poverty or persistent poverty only had managed only approximately a quarter of the level of average monthly savings of those in either of the short-term poverty states.

Among children whose parents managed to save at all during the five years, the average amounts saved during the years in which savings were made were quite high, even among children in the worst poverty states: an average of £41.55 per month among the parents of children in persistent poverty only and £53.74 among those in persistent and severe poverty (not a significant difference between these two groups). However, these levels were much lower than among the parents of children in the two short-term poverty states (£75.34 and £70.74) or among those who had experienced no poverty (£100.89).

12.3.2 Debt

One way in which parents can attempt to cushion children's poverty is to go into debt, although qualitative research findings have suggested that poor families are deeply reluctant to get into debt, using credit only as a last resort (Middleton, 2002). It might be predicted that the longer that children spend in poverty, the more likely parents will be to have recourse to debt. Indeed, Chapter 11 of this report has already shown that children in persistent poverty (with or without severity) were more likely than other children to live in households that were behind with housing payments and with the payment of other household bills.

Parents were asked whether they currently owed money in seven areas (see Table 12.3) in Wave 5 only, so that the following analysis compares children's poverty status by parents' experiences of debt in just that one year. It should be remembered that this does not necessarily reflect their experiences in all other years for which poverty has been measured.

In terms of the extent to which parents currently owed money, there were few differences between children in the five poverty categories. With the exception of children in persistent poverty only (62 per cent – a significantly greater proportion than children in persistent and severe poverty[2]), just over half of children in the four remaining categories had parents who owed money at the time they were interviewed in Wave 5 (Figure 12.5).

However, the **nature** of the debt that parents had incurred differed between children in the different poverty categories (Table 12.3). Children in persistent and severe poverty (37 per cent), and persistent poverty only (44 per cent), were far more likely than children who were in no poverty (22 per cent) to have parents who owed money for mail order purchases, which often cost more

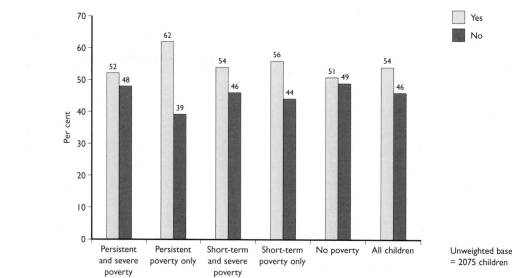

Figure 12.5 Parents who owe money by child's poverty status

Unweighted base = 2075 children

than goods bought from other sources. The higher cost of mail order purchase is particularly the case for shopping catalogues that are popular with poorer families because they allow the cost of goods to be repaid over time and charge no interest. On the other hand, children in the two persistent poverty states were far less likely to have parents who owed money on credit cards than those in any of the other states. Children in persistent poverty only were by far the most likely to have parents who owed money for a Social Fund loan. Differences in the use of other forms of loan were relatively small.

In terms of the number of debts that parents had – ie, in how many of the seven areas analysed above they owed money – children in persistent and severe poverty (41 per cent), those in persistent poverty only (40 per cent) and those in short-term and severe poverty (45 per cent) were more likely than children who experienced no poverty (31 per cent) to have parents with just

one debt (Table 12.4, overleaf). Children in persistent and severe poverty (11 per cent), and those in short-term and severe poverty (9 per cent), were far less likely to have parents with two or more debts than children in any of the other states, around a fifth of whom had parents with two or more debts.

The amount owed by parents on the seven items of debt also varied significantly by the poverty status of their children, with levels of debt **lower** the worse the poverty status of the children (Figure 12.6, overleaf). Including children whose parents did not have any debts, children in persistent and severe poverty had parents who owed, on average, £276.22 compared with £903.02 for children who had experienced no poverty.

The pattern was the same when only children whose parents had any debts were analysed, with the parents of children in persistent and severe

Table 12.3 Who parents currently owe money to by child's poverty status

Cell per cent

	Persistent and severe poverty	Persistent poverty only	Short-term and severe poverty	Short-term poverty only	No poverty	All children
Hire purchase	(10)	14	(10)	12	15	14
Personal loan from bank, building society or other financial institution*	13	10	(12)	19	18	16
Credit cards*	(3)	7	(19)	16	20	15
Mail order purchase*	37	44	(21)	33	22	29
DSS Social Fund loan*	(4)	13	(2)	(2)	(<0.5)	3
Loans from individual	(2)	(3)	(2)	(2)	2	2
Something else	0	(1)	(2)	(1)	(<0.5)	(1)

*significant differences (p<0.05)   Unweighted base = 2073 children

Table 12.4 Number of debts parents had by child's poverty status

Column per cent

	Persistent and severe poverty	Persistent poverty only	Short-term and severe poverty	Short-term poverty only	No poverty	All children
None	48	39	46	44	49	46
One	41	40	45	34	31	35
Two or more	11	21	(9)	21	20	19

Unweighted base = 2073 children

Figure 12.6 Average amount parents owed by child's poverty status[3]

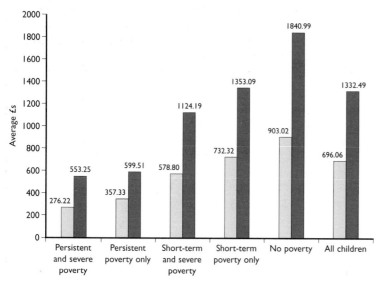

Unweighted base = 2019 (all children) and 1065 (children whose parents owe money)

poverty owing an average of £553.25 and those with no poverty £1840.99. Interestingly, as a proportion of current net weekly income, the figures for all states were not significantly different (with the exception of children in short-term and severe poverty whose parents' debts as a proportion of income were significantly higher than for the other poverty states). In other words, as a proportion of their income, parents owed approximately the same amount.

12.4 Parents' emotional well-being

The ability of parents to deal with life on a low income is likely to be undermined if they are not supported in their day-to-day lives and/or if their mental health is suffering as a consequence. It might be anticipated that these, in turn, will affect the lives of their children. This section considers the emotional well-being of parents by investigating the levels of support they believed they would receive in certain situations and their mental health.

12.4.1 Parents' levels of support

Parents were asked whether, in five different situations, they would expect to receive support from one person, more than one person or no one. As with the civic organisation questions, responses have been analysed for either the last or penultimate wave that the children were in the sample.

Overall, the levels of support anticipated by children's parents were approximately the same for each situation: just under two-fifths of all children had parents who felt they would receive support from one person; a little under three-fifths anticipated support from more than one person; while levels of expecting no support ranged from just 3 per cent to 5 per cent (Table 12.5).

Table 12.5 Support parents expected to receive by child's poverty status

Column per cent within each category

	Persistent and severe poverty	Persistent poverty only	Short-term and severe poverty	Short-term poverty only	No poverty	All children
Someone who will listen						
Yes, one person	37	42	42	39	37	39
Yes, more than one	54	49	57	59	61	58
No one	(9)	9	(2)	(2)	2	4
Someone to help in crisis						
Yes, one person	33	44	43	33	37	38
Yes, more than one	56	47	55	63	62	58
No one	(11)	8	(2)	(4)	2	4
Someone you can relax with						
Yes, one person	37	42	39	38	39	39
Yes, more than one	52	53	61	60	59	58
No one	(11)	(6)	0	(2)	(2)	3
Someone who really appreciates you						
Yes, one person	32	35	37	33	32	33
Yes, more than one	59	55	58	62	64	61
No one	(10)	10	(5)	(5)	3	5
Someone you can count on for comfort						
Yes, one person	30	47	43	36	38	39
Yes, more than one	58	45	55	61	60	57
No one	(12)	8	(2)	(4)	3	5

Unweighted base = 2063–2069 children (differences due to missing values)

However, there were differences according to poverty state. Although numbers were small, it appears that children in persistent poverty, with or without severity, were much more likely than children in the other three states to have parents who reported that they had no one's support in each of the situations, in most cases around four times more likely. For support to provide 'help in a crisis' and for 'comfort', it appears that children in persistent and severe poverty were more likely than children in persistent poverty only to have parents who had the support of more than one person. The only significant difference between children in persistent and severe poverty and in persistent poverty only were that children in the former were more likely to have parents without anybody they could count on for comfort.

In order to summarise the differences between poverty groups, the number of situations in which parents had no support were summed (Figure 12.7). Overall the majority of children had parents with support in all situations (89 per cent), but this did vary somewhat by poverty status. Children in persistent poverty, with or without severity, were more likely to have parents lacking support in one situation (8 per cent and 10 per cent, respectively) or two or more situations (14 and 11 per cent, respectively). These figures contrast starkly to those for other children, among whom around one in 20 lacked support in one situation and approximately one in 30 in two or more situations.

Figure 12.7 Number of areas in which parents lacked support by child's poverty status

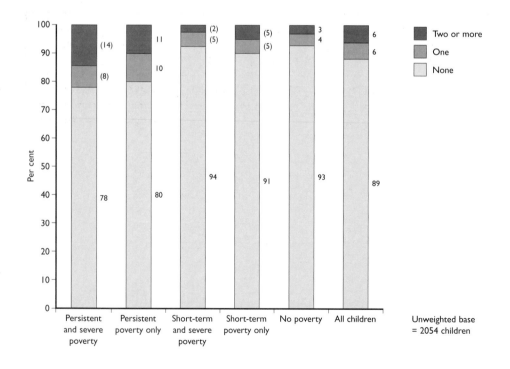

12.4.2 Mental health

It might be expected that the multiple strains of life on a low income, problems with the home and lower levels of support would result in poorer emotional well-being for parents. Indeed, Part 1 found that parents' General Health Questionnaire (GHQ) scores rose (worsened) the more severe the child's poverty.

The BHPS also includes a GHQ measure which, although calculated slightly differently to the measure used in Part 1, is based on the same 12 questions (regarding respondents' feelings about their concentration, ability to sleep, general happiness and so on). The difference is that in the BHPS a respondent is given a score of zero for the least distressed answer and three for the most distressed (in the PSE the respective scores were one and four). These scores are then added together for the 12 questions to produce a GHQ score, so the lowest (best) possible score, in this case, is zero and the highest (worst) possible score is 36.

The average GHQ score of parents (averaged over the five-year period) was significantly greater (worse) for children in persistent and severe poverty and persistent poverty only than for other children (Table 12.6). In other words, children in persistent poverty, with or without severity, were more likely to have parents who were the most distressed on the 12 measures than other children's parents.

Table 12.6 Parents' average GHQ score over five years by child's poverty status[4]

Column per cent

	Persistent and severe poverty	Persistent poverty only	Short-term and severe poverty	Short-term poverty only	No poverty	All children
Average GHQ score	13.3771	13.1701	12.3926	12.1488	11.4996	12.1430

Unweighted base = 1979 children

13 Persistent and severe poverty in childhood and young people's social exclusion

The previous two chapters have described associations between the persistence and severity of a child's poverty and the social exclusion experiences of their households and parents. Since 1994 the BHPS has also included a Youth Questionnaire that, among other things, collects information about some of young people's experiences which might be related to young people's 'exclusion'. This chapter first describes the sample used in analysing responses to these questions, which differs from those in previous sections, and then compares these experiences for young people in each of the poverty states. The analysis focuses on four main areas of young people's potential exclusion:

- relationships with friends and family
- pocket money and part-time work
- school experiences and career aspirations
- emotional well-being.

13.1 Young people included in the Youth Questionnaire

The BHPS Youth Questionnaire is administered to young people between the ages of 11 and 15 and, as noted above, only began in 1994. This means that not all the children in our sample had answered this questionnaire at all, or had answered it in only a limited number of years. Therefore, analysis in this chapter only includes young people in the third cohort, those aged 10–14 years, and focuses on their responses to the Youth Questionnaire at the age of 14 years. In this way, the exclusion experiences of these young people are being compared after they have potentially experienced poverty persistence and/or severity over the five-year period. When the BHPS and the Youth Questionnaire have been running for a longer period of time it will be possible, and of great interest, to investigate if, and how, young people's experiences change according to their changing experiences of poverty. At this stage, however, this more limited analysis – what might be seen as a 'demonstration' of the future potential of the youth data – is all that has been possible.

The fact that we are working with a much smaller sample than in previous chapters is highlighted in Table 13.1 which shows the number of young people in each of the poverty states. The smaller sample size means that results must be treated with some degree of caution (it will be noted that many of the results in this chapter are bracketed, meaning that they are based on less than 20 unweighted cases). There are far too few young people in short-term and severe poverty to allow conclusions to be drawn, so results have not been included for this group in the following analysis. The slightly different poverty rates when using only young people in the third cohort should also be noted.

13.2 Relationships with friends and family

It is possible that the experience of poverty in childhood, particularly when poverty is persistent and severe, could affect young people's relationships with both their friends and family.

Table 13.1 Persistent and severe poverty: young people aged 10–14 years

	Percentage of young people	Unweighted number of young people
No poverty	53	286
Short-term poverty only	16	80
Short-term and severe poverty	(2)	10
Persistent poverty only	21	86
Persistent and severe poverty	8	42

Unweighted base = 504 young people

For example, the maintenance of friendships might be more difficult for poor young people if, as was shown in Part 1 of this report, their families are unable to afford for them to participate in social activities or to have 'friends round for tea' on a regular basis. Within the family, it might be expected that poverty could strain relationships between young people and their parents, particularly if the parents of poor young people are more likely to experience mental health problems, as has been suggested in Part 1 of the report and in the previous chapter.

13.2.1 Friendship

Young people were asked a number of questions about their relationships with friends, including the number of close friends they had, how often they saw them, how often they got into fights and how happy they were with their friendships.

There was little difference in the average number of close friends that young people had according to poverty status; all reported an average of between six and seven close friends (figures not shown).

However, it seems that young people who had experienced persistent and severe poverty were less likely to have had friends round to visit at all in the past week (38 per cent), than each of the other groups of young people (approximately a quarter in each case had not had friends round to visit) (Table 13.2, overleaf). In contrast, it seems that young people who were in persistent poverty only (42 per cent) were more likely than young people in persistent and severe poverty or in no poverty (25 per cent and 31 per cent, respectively) to have had friends visit on three or more occasions in the past week. Although this evidence is far from conclusive, it may be that parents manage to afford hospitality for their young people's friends even if poverty is persistent, but are unable to do so when poverty becomes severe. Alternatively, it may be that some of these young people were choosing to meet their friends out of the home, rather than in it, to avoid the possibility that hospitality could not be provided.

Three in ten young people reported that they had been in a fight one or more times in the past

Table 13.2 Number of times friends have visited house in past seven days by poverty status

Column per cent

	Persistent and severe poverty	Persistent poverty only	Short-term poverty only	No poverty	All young people
None	(38)	25	(22)	28	28
1 – 2	(38)	33	41	41	39
3 or more	(25)	42	37	31	34

Unweighted base = 489 young people

Table 13.3 Number of times been in a fight in the past month by poverty status

Column per cent

	Persistent and severe poverty	Persistent poverty only	Short-term poverty only	No poverty	All young people
Never	72	69	68	71	70
Once or more	(28)	31	32	29	30

Unweighted base = 489 young people

month (30 per cent) (Table 13.3). The proportion was approximately the same regardless of young people's poverty status.

In a wider exploration of satisfaction with their lives, young people were asked how happy they were about their friends. They could answer on a scale of 1 'completely happy' to 7 'completely unhappy'. For the purposes of this analysis young people who said that they were happy to any degree (that is, 1–3 on the scale) were coded as happy and those who were unhappy to any degree (that is, 5–7 on the scale) were coded as unhappy.

Nearly all young people (94 per cent) were happy with their friends (Figure 13.1). This varied very little by poverty status with, if anything, young people in persistent and severe poverty the most likely to be happy with their friends.

13.2.2 Family relationships
Young people were asked how often they argued with their mum and their dad, and how often they talked to them 'about things that matter'.[1]

Just over a fifth of all young people argued with their dad regularly, that is, on most days or more than once a week (22 per cent), compared to just over three in ten who argued with their mum regularly (31 per cent) (Figure 13.2).

Figure 13.1 Happiness with friends by poverty status

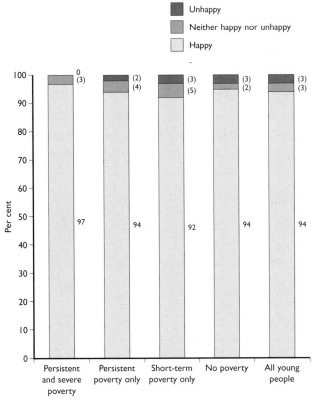

Unweighted base = 488 young people

Figure 13.2 Regularly argue with mum and dad by poverty status

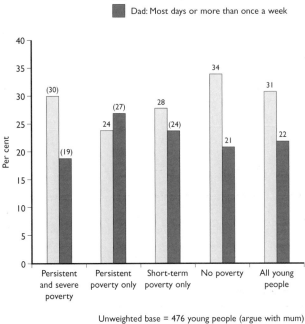

Unweighted base = 476 young people (argue with mum)
and 372 young people (argue with dad)

Young people who had experienced any degree of poverty were slightly less likely to say they argued regularly with their mum than were young people in no poverty (34 per cent). This was particularly the case for young people in persistent poverty only (24 per cent), who were also the only young people less likely to argue with their mum than their dad. The opposite appeared to be the case for arguing with dad. With the exception of young people in persistent and severe poverty, slightly more young people who experienced poverty argued with their dad on a regular basis than young people who had experienced no poverty.

In addition to being slightly more likely to argue regularly with their mum than with their dad, young people were also twice as likely to talk to their mum as to their dad about things that mattered to them on most days or more than once a week (48 compared to 24 per cent) (Figure 13.3, overleaf). But the extent to which young people talked to either parent varied far more by poverty experience than it did in the case of arguing. Young people who had experienced no poverty were more likely to discuss things on a regular basis with their parents than young people who had experienced any degree of poverty. Young people in persistent and severe poverty were the least likely to talk about things that matter to either their mum or dad (36 and 12 per cent, respectively). This may be because they were well aware of their parents' stressful lives and did not want to add to their parents' problems, as qualitative work with children has suggested (Ridge, 2002).

Young people were also asked how happy they felt with their family life and the results were coded in the same way as described above for friends.

Generally young people were happy with their families: almost nine-tenths of all young people (89 per cent) (Figure 13.4). This proportion was similar for all groups of young people with the exception of those in persistent and severe poverty. These young people were much less likely to be happy with their families (just 70 per cent). This can perhaps be attributed to the greater transitions that had taken place in the families of young people who experienced persistent and severe poverty compared to other young people (as seen in Chapter 10).

Figure 13.3 Regularly talk to mum and dad about things that matter by poverty status

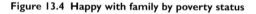

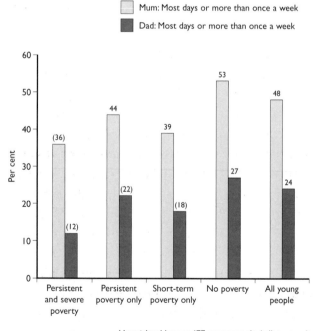

Unweighted base = 477 young people (talk to mum) and 392 young people (talk to dad)

Figure 13.4 Happy with family by poverty status

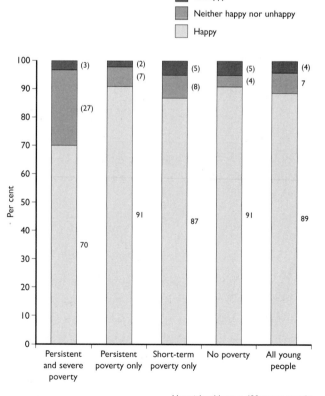

Unweighted base = 488 young people

13.3 Pocket money and part-time work

There is some evidence that young people (aged 10 to 16) from poorer families and those from more affluent families have different experiences of receiving pocket money and of earning money from part-time work outside the home. In general, it seems that poor young people are less likely to receive regular pocket money and, when they do, receive lower amounts (Shropshire and Middleton, 1999). Similarly, poor young people are less likely to work part-time but, when they do, they work for longer hours and for lower rates of pay (Middleton and Loumidis, 2001). There are some questions in the Youth Questionnaire that allow these findings to be explored with this cohort of young people.

13.3.1 Pocket money
Nine-tenths of young people had received pocket money in the previous week (88 per cent). It appears that young people in persistent and severe poverty were the least likely to have received pocket money in the last week; just three-quarters did so (73 per cent) (figures not shown).

Among all young people who had received pocket money in the previous week, the average was £9.27. However, it seems that when young people did receive pocket money, those in persistent and severe poverty had received the lowest amount (£6.46) and those in persistent poverty only had received the largest amount (£11.35) (Figure 13.5). This finding is somewhat strange and we have no immediate explanation.

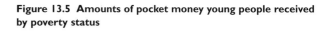

Figure 13.5 Amounts of pocket money young people received by poverty status

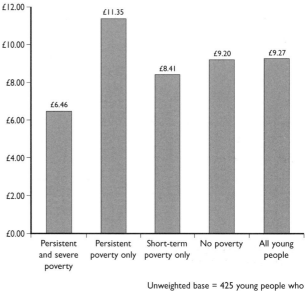

Unweighted base = 425 young people who received pocket money

13.3.2 Paid part-time work
Two-fifths of young people were undertaking paid part-time work. Broadly confirming the findings of earlier research, young people who had experienced persistent poverty, with or without severity (31 and 30 per cent respectively), were less likely to have had a part-time job than young people in short-term poverty only or no poverty (44 and 42 per cent respectively) (Table 13.4, overleaf). The reasons why poorer young people are less likely to work part-time remain speculative. It may be that these young people live in areas where part-time work is less likely to be available, and/or that many young people access part-time jobs through their parents' work contacts, which will not be available to poor young people with parents who do not have a job (Middleton and Loumidis, 2001).

Table 13.4 Part-time paid work by poverty status

Column per cent

	Persistent and severe poverty	Persistent poverty only	Short-term poverty only	No poverty	All young people
No	69	70	57	58	61
Yes	(31)	30	44	42	39

Unweighted base = 483 young people

Table 13.5 Average number of hours worked and hourly wage among young people who worked by poverty status

	Persistent and severe poverty	Persistent poverty only	Short-term poverty only	No poverty	All young people
Average number of hours worked	(3.7)	5.6	6.6	6.4	6.1
Average hourly earnings	(£1.87)	£2.40	£2.50	£2.56	£2.48

Unweighted base = 192 young people (hours worked) and 190 young people (earnings)

It appears that not only were young people in persistent poverty less likely to work, but also when they did work, their hours of work were shorter on average than those of other young people (Table 13.5). The hourly earnings of young people who had experienced poverty also appeared to be lower than those of young people who had experienced no poverty, again confirming the findings of earlier research (Middleton and Loumidis, 2001).

13.4 School experiences and career aspirations

Part 1 suggested that young people who experienced (severe) poverty had more negative school experiences than those who were not poor, in terms of experiences of bullying and suspensions from school. The Youth Questionnaire includes a range of questions about school experiences, including suspensions and exclusions from school, truanting, bullying, relationships with teachers, attitudes to schoolwork and parents' involvement with school. Unfortunately, most of these were only asked from Wave 7 (1997) onwards and so cannot be included in this analysis. However, it is worth noting that a cross-sectional analysis of these data was undertaken by Ridge (2002) and, in summary, showed that poor young people (defined as those in families in receipt of Income Support or Jobseeker's Allowance), fared worse on most of these measures than young people who were not poor. These data have immense future potential for a comparison of poverty and educational experiences over time.

However, this analysis is confined to looking at five questions:

- the extent to which young people worried about being bullied at school
- their views on the importance of doing well at school
- how happy they felt with their school work
- their intentions about whether to stay on in education after they are 16 years old
- their career aspirations.

13.4.1 Worrying about bullying

Part 1 found that severely poor children were more likely to have been bullied than other children, as reported by their parents. Data from the Youth Questionnaire allows an analysis of the extent to which young people themselves worried about the prospect of being bullied.

In general, young people who had experienced poverty were no more likely than young people with no experience of poverty to be 'a lot' or 'a bit' worried about bullying, although those in persistent poverty only were five percentage points more likely to be worried than those in no poverty (Table 13.6). However, the BHPS question differed in a number of ways from the PSE question. The latter asked whether young people *had been* bullied; the question was asked of parents not young people and the analysis covered all children, not just those aged 14 years.

13.4.2 Importance of doing well at school

Sixty-three per cent of all young people said that it meant a great deal to them to do well at school, 33 per cent responded that it meant quite a lot, 3 per cent not very much and just 1 per cent very little. The last three categories

Table 13.6 Worrying about being bullied by poverty status

Column per cent

	Persistent and severe poverty	Persistent poverty only	Short-term poverty only	No poverty	All young people
A lot or a bit	(34)	38	29	33	34
Not at all	66	62	71	67	66

Unweighted base = 488 young people

have been combined for this analysis because of small numbers.

It is encouraging that young people who had experienced poverty were only slightly less likely to say that doing well at school meant a great deal to them than young people who had experienced no poverty (Table 13.7). However, young people who had experienced short-term poverty only appeared slightly less likely to say that it meant a great deal to them. It is not clear why this should be the case.

13.4.3 Happy with school work

Young people were asked how happy they felt about their school work, and their responses were coded as happy, neither happy nor unhappy, or unhappy.

More than four-fifths of young people were happy with their school work (Figure 13.6). This proportion was found for all young people with the exception of young people in persistent and severe poverty, among whom a larger proportion (26 per cent) were unhappy or neither happy nor unhappy with their school work than was the case for other young people (between 16 and 19 per cent).

Figure 13.6 Happy with school work by poverty status

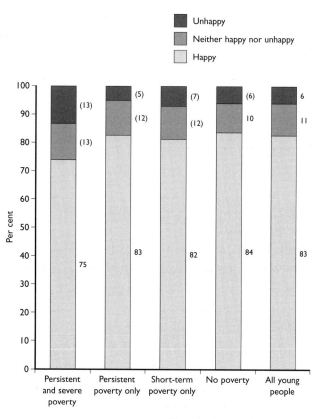

Unweighted base = 488 young people

Table 13.7 How much it means to do well at school by poverty status

Column per cent

	Persistent and severe poverty	Persistent poverty only	Short-term poverty only	No poverty	All young people
A great deal	63	61	53	66	63
Quite a lot or less	(38)	39	47	34	37

Unweighted base = 488 young people

Table 13.8 Stay on at school after 16 by poverty status

Column per cent

	Persistent and severe poverty	Persistent poverty only	Short-term poverty only	No poverty	All young people
Yes	72	59	69	81	74
No	(16)	(14)	(16)	(7)	11
Undecided	(13)	27	(15)	12	15

Unweighted base = 488 young people

13.4.4 Staying on in education

Seventy-four per cent of young people said that they would go on to sixth form or college when they were 16, 11 per cent said that they would leave school and 15 per cent were undecided (Table 13.8).

Young people who had experienced no poverty (81 per cent) were more likely than young people who had experienced any degree of poverty to say that they would stay on at school. This was particularly the case for young people in persistent poverty only; less than three-fifths of these young people said that they would stay on at school (59 per cent) while over a quarter were undecided about their choice (27 per cent).

At first sight it seems peculiar that young people in persistent and severe poverty were more likely to say that they would stay in education after 16 (72 per cent) than young people in persistent poverty only (59 per cent), but a review of other findings so far provides a possible explanation. Section 10.1.7 showed that the parents of children in persistent and severe poverty were more likely to have higher educational

qualifications than children in persistent poverty only and this may, perhaps, have influenced their children's decisions regarding further education.

13.4.5 Career aspirations

Earlier cross-sectional research has suggested that poorer young people have lower career aspirations than young people from more affluent families (Shropshire and Middleton, 1999). The Youth Questionnaire asked young people what job they would like when they left school. However, this question was asked only up until Wave 8. Therefore, young people who were aged 14 in Wave 9 could not be analysed.

The survey classified young people's responses into the Standard Occupational Classification which includes nine major occupational groups. For the purposes of our analysis these have been further collapsed into just four groups[2] (Table 13.9, overleaf).

The findings, while less stark than those of Shropshire and Middleton, give some indication of lower career aspirations among poor young people, particularly those in persistent poverty

Table 13.9 Career aspirations by poverty status

Column per cent

	Persistent and severe poverty	Persistent poverty only	Short-term poverty only	No poverty	All young people
Professional/managerial	(32)	(14)	(22)	27	24
Skilled occupation	(20)	40	41	40	39
Unskilled manual	(31)	38	(23)	22	26
Other	(17)	(8)	(15)	12	12

Unweighted base = 391 young people

only, than among young people who experienced no poverty. Just 14 per cent of young people in persistent poverty only aspired to a professional or managerial career, compared with 27 per cent of young people in no poverty. At the other end of the scale, 38 per cent of young people in persistent poverty only intended to enter an unskilled manual occupation compared with 22 per cent of young people in no poverty.

13.5 Emotional well-being

Finally in this chapter we examine relationships between young people's experiences of poverty and a number of measures that can broadly be described as capturing young people's feelings of 'emotional well-being': their happiness, loneliness, self-worth, and satisfaction with their appearance and life as a whole.

13.5.1 Unhappiness
Although 71 per cent of all young people reported having felt 'unhappy on at least one day in the previous month', it seems that young people in

poverty were no more likely to have felt unhappy than young people in no poverty (Table 13.10). In fact, it appears that young people in persistent and severe poverty were more likely to say they had not felt unhappy at all in the past month (38 per cent) than young people in no poverty (29 per cent).

13.5.2 Loneliness
A relatively high proportion of young people reported that they felt lonely at least occasionally (43 per cent) (Table 13.11). It appears that young people in persistent poverty, with or without severity, were twice as likely to experience loneliness very or quite often (both 16 per cent) as young people who experienced no poverty (8 per cent). However, the two most serious poverty groups were less likely to have experienced loneliness occasionally.

13.5.3 Feelings of self-worth
It might be anticipated that the experience of poverty could undermine young people's sense of their own value. This is explored in the Youth Questionnaire through a number of attitude

statements to which young people are asked to respond: strongly agree, agree, disagree or strongly disagree. For this analysis, these responses have been collapsed simply into whether the young person agreed or disagreed with each statement because of the small sample size (Table 13.12, overleaf).

For four out of the five statements it seems that persistent poverty, with or without severity, was associated with lower feelings of self-worth. This was particularly the case for feeling 'useless at times' and being 'inclined to feel a failure'. Two-fifths of young people in persistent poverty only and over a half in persistent and severe

poverty felt useless at times compared to over a third of young people in no poverty. In the case of being inclined to feel a failure, young people in persistent poverty only were one-and-a-half times more likely to agree (12 per cent), than young people in no poverty (8 per cent), and those in persistent and severe poverty twice as likely to do so (16 per cent).

Reassuringly, a very high proportion of young people agreed that they are 'a likeable person' (96 per cent), and for this statement, poverty did not seem to be associated with lower levels of self-esteem.

Table 13.10 How many days felt unhappy in the past month

Column per cent

	Persistent and severe poverty	Persistent poverty only	Short-term poverty only	No poverty	All young people
None	(38)	26	31	29	29
1–3	(41)	46	52	48	47
4 or more	(22)	28	(18)	24	24

Unweighted base = 488 young people

Table 13.11 How often feel lonely by poverty status

Column per cent

	Persistent and severe poverty	Persistent poverty only	Short-term poverty only	No poverty	All young people
Very or quite often	(16)	(16)	(5)	8	10
Occasionally	(31)	20	36	38	33
Hardly ever	53	64	60	53	57

Unweighted base = 487 young people

Table 13.12 Self-worth by poverty status

Column per cent

Proportion who agree to the following remarks	Persistent and severe poverty	Persistent poverty only	Short-term poverty only	No poverty	All young people
I feel I have a number of good qualities	88	87	92	94	92
I am a likeable person	94	94	95	96	96
I certainly feel useless at times	(55)	42	32	36	38
I am inclined to feel that I am a failure	(16)	(12)	(5)	8	9
At times I feel that I am no good	(31)	34	31	26	29

Unweighted base = 484–488 young people (differences due to missing values)

13.5.4 Satisfaction with appearance and life as a whole

In the investigation of areas of life with which young people were happy, along with their school work, family and friends, young people were asked about their happiness with their appearance and their life as a whole. These were coded in the same way as described in earlier sections.

Three-quarters of all young people felt happy with their appearance (76 per cent) (Figure 13.7). A slightly greater proportion of young people who were in persistent poverty only were happy (81 per cent), but young people who were in persistent and severe poverty were the least likely to be happy. Just two-thirds of these young people were happy with their appearance, and a large proportion were neither happy nor unhappy (25 per cent).

Nearly nine-tenths of all young people were happy with their lives as a whole (87 per cent) (Figure 13.8). Young people in persistent poverty, with or without severity, were the least likely to be happy with their lives as a whole, but this was particularly the case for young people in persistent and severe poverty (70 per cent).

Figure 13.7 Happy with appearance by poverty status

Figure 13.8 Happy with life as a whole by poverty status

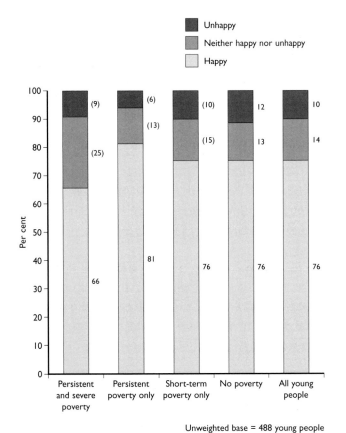

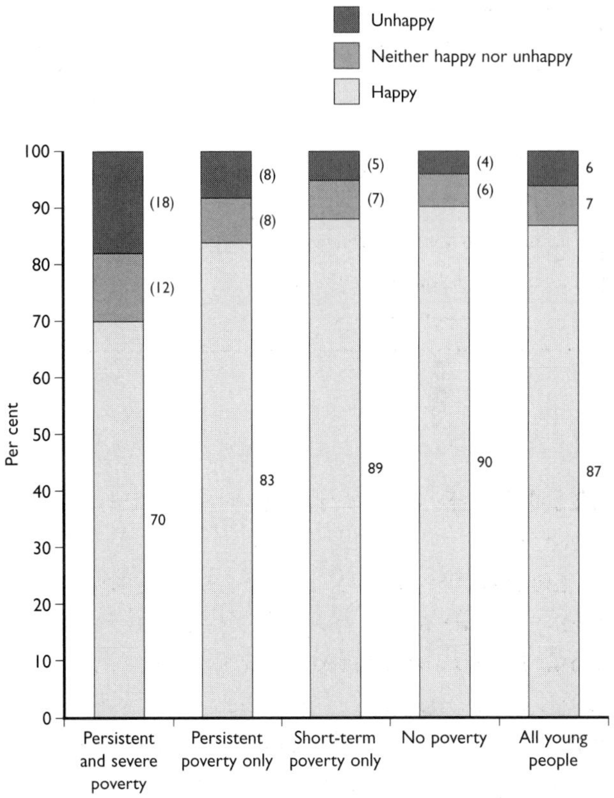

Unweighted base = 488 young people

Unweighted base = 488 young people

14 Summary of key findings

The aim of Part 2 of the report was to use an income measure of severe child poverty to track children's poverty experiences over a number of years, in particular to analyse the persistence of severe poverty for children.

14.1 Definition and measurement

At present, there is no single data source that measures income, child deprivation and adult deprivation over time, so that the definition of severe child poverty used in Part 1 of the report could not be used to analyse persistent and severe poverty. Therefore, an income definition had to be used for the measurement of persistent poverty but, for consistency, severe and non-severe poverty thresholds were created by determining the median income of children experiencing severe and non-severe poverty, as defined by the income poverty and deprivation measure in Part 1. These equated to 27 per cent and 59 per cent of weekly median household income, respectively.

Using the BHPS for the years 1991–1999, children were analysed over a five-year period (between the ages of 0–4 years, 5–9 years, 10–14 years and 15–19 years). For each of the five years it was calculated whether children were in severe, non-severe or no poverty.

Persistent poverty was defined as occurring when children experienced poverty (severe or non-severe) in three out of the five years for which they were analysed – this affected 29 per cent of children. Severe poverty was defined as occurring if children experienced severe poverty in at least one of the five years – 13 per cent of children experienced at least one year of severe poverty. Using these criteria, five poverty persistence and severity groups were established:

- no poverty – not in poverty in any of the five years
- short-term poverty only – less than three years in poverty and no years in severe poverty
- short-term and severe poverty – less than three years in poverty but at least one year in severe poverty
- persistent poverty only – three or more years in poverty but no years in severe poverty
- persistent and severe poverty – three or more years in poverty and at least one year in severe poverty.

Nine per cent of British children were estimated to have experienced persistent and severe poverty over the five-year period for which they were studied.

14.2 Which children were in persistent and severe poverty?

Children who experienced **any form of poverty** over the five-year period were different in a number of ways from children who never experienced poverty. Children experiencing poverty were all **more** likely (when all other characteristics were held constant) to have:
- been in a no worker household for one year
- lived in rented accommodation for five years
- had adults in the household who were ill for between three and four years
- lived in the Midlands
- received benefits for three or four years and
- lived in a household with an average of three or more children.

In addition, children in poverty were all **less** likely to have had parents educated to degree level than children never in poverty.

Characteristics that distinguished children who experienced both **persistent and severe poverty** from children in persistent poverty only were that children in persistent and severe poverty were significantly **less** likely to have:

- been in a lone parent family for five years
- lived in a household which never had work as a main source of annual income (measured in the year prior to the interview) and
- lived in a household which moved between no worker and two workers (or vice versa).

They were **more** likely to have lived in a household which had:

- no workers in all years (measured at the time of interview)
- two or more transitions in their main source of income
- an average of three or more children in the household
- parents educated to degree or A level.

It appears that there were at least two distinct groups of children in persistent and severe poverty as defined by their family's work and benefit characteristics.

1 The first group were those whose financial situation appeared relatively stable, although very bleak. This group included children who had lived in workless households for all of the five-year period and who were also most likely to have spent all five years dependent on benefits as a main income source, further increasing their chances of persistent and severe poverty.

2 The second group were those who experienced income volatility, ie, two or more income transitions between work/other income and benefit income as their main source of income. Children whose households underwent two or more such transitions were much more likely to be in persistent and severe poverty than children who did not experience these transitions. As these children experiencing multiple changes in their main source of income must also have spent at least one year in receipt of benefits, it is likely that their actual chances of experiencing persistent and severe poverty were compounded further.

Children in persistent and severe poverty were **less** likely to have spent all of the five-year period in a lone parent family. This is not to say that children in lone parent families were missing from the group in persistent and severe poverty. Rather, that once their other circumstances were taken into account, children in stable lone parents families were less likely to face persistent and severe poverty than children who constantly lived in a couple family.

14.3 Which children were socially excluded?

Reflecting the available measures in the BHPS, social exclusion was measured from three different perspectives:

- exclusion experiences that would affect the whole household

- parents' experiences of exclusion that were also likely to impact on the child
- the young person's own exclusion experiences at the age of 14 years.

In general, on the **household measures of exclusion** all children in poverty, whatever its persistence or severity, fared much worse than children who had not experienced poverty in any of the five years. There was a very slight trend for children in persistent poverty, with or without severity, to be more likely to have been excluded on a minority of measures (namely to have experienced some financial difficulties, to lack commonly owned consumer durables and to lack 'necessities' because they could not be afforded), but, in general, differences between the poverty groups were small.

However, a much clearer divide between the poverty groups was seen on the measures of **parents' experiences of exclusion**. Once again, in general, children in any form of poverty were more likely to have parents who had experienced exclusion than children never in poverty, but children in persistent poverty, with or without severity, were more likely than the other poverty groups to have parents who had done so. The parents of children in persistent poverty, whether or not the poverty was severe, were **less** likely to:

- be satisfied with the neighbourhood in which they lived
- be engaged in civic activity (for example voting or active membership of organisations)
- be able to save or to save as much
- have high levels of emotional well-being.

An analysis of the **social exclusion experiences of children** at the age of 14 (based on their poverty persistence and severity between the ages of 10 and 14) suggested that young people experiencing poverty were no worse off in terms of:

- their relationships and satisfaction with friends
- their experiences at school
- their level of belief that they were a likeable person.

However, they did seem to be affected by life on a low income in other ways. Young people in persistent and severe poverty:

- received the lowest level of pocket money
- along with young people in persistent poverty only, were the least likely to have part-time jobs and, when they did so, worked fewer hours and for less money than other young people
- appeared more likely to have strained relationships with their parents; they were least likely to talk to their parents about things that mattered or to be happy with their family
- were least likely to be happy with their appearance and, indeed, with their life as a whole.

Young people appear to be very much affected, at least in some aspects of their lives, by their experiences of poverty. This highlights the importance of being concerned with the impact of poverty on children's current lives **as children**, not just because of the effects poverty may have on children's future experiences as adults (as so much research seems to do).

Part 3 Implications for Britain's poorest children

15 Policy implications

The Labour government, first elected in 1997, has made a commitment to ending child poverty within 20 years, halving it within 10 years and reducing it by at least a quarter by 2004. Currently child poverty is most often measured as children in households with incomes below 60 per cent of contemporary median income and, as the government itself has said, 'In the absence of a single official measure of poverty, low income... often becomes a default headline measure' (Department for Work and Pensions, 2003b, p.1)[1]. At the time of writing, preliminary conclusions to the government's consultation on how child poverty should be measured have just been released (ibid.). These propose further work on poverty measures in addition to income, including material deprivation, as well as other possible dimensions of childhood exclusion. With this in mind, this chapter discusses the policy implications that can be drawn from both parts of this report and the important lessons it contains for both measuring and tackling child poverty.

15.1 Monitoring policy

A range of policies has been implemented in order to meet the government's child poverty targets, focusing on paid work for parents as the main solution to the problem of child poverty. These include Child Tax Credit (which replaced all pre-existing cash benefits for children except Child Benefit in April 2003), Working Tax Credit, Childcare Tax Credit and the National Minimum Wage.

The government has also committed itself to providing more opportunities for children and young people to be 'involved in the design, provision and evaluation of policies and services that affect them or which they use' (Children and Young People's Unit, 2001a, p.2). This can, and should, **involve children in the development of strategies for the reduction of poverty and social exclusion**. Indeed, the *Measuring Child Poverty* consultation included a number of workshops with children in which they 'described the exclusion experienced by children living in poverty and the essentials that they felt children could not live without' (Department for Work and Pensions, 2003b, p.9). Interestingly, the majority of the goods, services and other areas mentioned by children have been analysed in this report (ibid. p.16).

Data in Part 1 of this report were collected in 1999, and data in Part 2 between 1991 and 1999, before most of the policies outlined above were (fully) implemented, so it is unlikely that their effects will be seen in these analyses. The first, and most obvious, implication of this report is, therefore, the **need to monitor the effects of these policy initiatives on levels of severe and persistent poverty** as further waves of data from the BHPS and other longitudinal datasets become available. The effect of these changes for the income and deprivation measure of severe poverty used in Part 1 cannot be tested unless the PSE survey is replicated[2] (further implications for the measurement of child poverty are discussed below). Nevertheless, a number of issues with important implications for policy have emerged from this report.

15.2 The extent and persistence of severe childhood poverty

In 1999, 8 per cent of children – that is, one in twelve – had experienced living in a household with less than 40 per cent of median income, and in which they themselves lacked at least one necessary item because it could not be afforded, and their parent(s) lacked two or more necessary items because they could not be afforded. Over a five-year period, 9 per cent of children had experienced income poverty that was persistent (three out of the five years with a household income below 59 per cent of the median) and severe (at least one year in a household with less than 27 per cent of median income). Thirteen per cent of children – one in eight – had experienced severe income poverty in at least one year out of five.

Severity is of concern for a number of reasons, not least for its apparent association with persistence and other manifestations of poverty and social exclusion that have been highlighted in both parts of this report. Within the context of target-driven policies, such as the reduction of child poverty by a quarter by 2004, there is a temptation to focus on those who are easiest to help, in this case children who are closest to the poverty line and, hence, easiest to move above it. However, for eradicating child poverty it would seem sensible to maintain a focus on dealing with children who are facing the most difficult circumstances, and to ensure that policy interventions benefit this group. One step forward, therefore, would be **to collect and publish official measures of severe poverty and to incorporate the aim of eliminating severe poverty, however defined, into official targets.**

15.3 Benefits

Children in need of urgent attention are those in households in **receipt of Income Support and Jobseeker's Allowance**. In Part 1 it was shown that children and parents in severe poverty, the large majority of whom were receiving these benefits, were going without many necessary items. In addition, the association between receiving these benefits and being in severe poverty remained significant, even when employment status and other characteristics were controlled for. In Part 2 it was found that periods spent in receipt of benefit were strongly associated with children experiencing some degree of income poverty and, again, this association remained significant when other characteristics were controlled for. This has at least two implications: families must take up their full entitlement to benefits and benefits must be adequate to keep children out of poverty.

15.3.1 Take-up of benefits

Greater emphasis needs to be placed on **ensuring that families receive all the benefits to which they are entitled** at the times they are entitled, so that they do not experience severe income poverty. The severe income poverty line in Part 2 of this report is lower than the Income Support levels – levels which are supposed to represent the minimum safety net for individuals and families in Britain. There are a number of possible reasons why children might have been living in households with incomes below these levels (as outlined in Chapter 8), and these need further investigation. However, it is worth highlighting the following possible explanations and their policy implications. First, households might not be receiving their (full) entitlement to benefits and increased efforts need to be made to improve levels of take-up.[3] Secondly, at the time when these data were collected it is possible that some of these children were in households on very low (part-time) wages. The introduction of the Minimum Wage, Working Families Tax Credit and, subsequently, Working and Child Tax Credits will have improved this situation (provided that families take up their entitlement), but this needs to be carefully monitored. Thirdly, making deductions at source from Income Support and Jobseeker's Allowance to repay, amongst other things, Social Fund loans needs urgent investigation.[4] It cannot be right that the government allows reductions in what it believes to be the minimum that a family needs to live on in order to repay these loans.

15.3.2 Benefit adequacy

At the time of the surveys it was clear that benefit levels were not sufficient for parents to protect their children from the effects of poverty. Parents should be able, at the very least, to afford necessities required by their children, such as fresh fruit and vegetables daily, to pay for their home, to keep their home in a good state of repair and to have adequate heating, to give just a few examples. **Benefits must be adequate to keep children out of poverty.**

15.4 Work

While both parts of this report have suggested that the government is right to urge work as the best protection from severe poverty and persistent poverty, there were still, in the years covered by these analyses at least, indications that **work did not always protect from poverty**. This was particularly the case for households where there was only one worker. In many such households one worker will be all that is possible because, for example, the household is a lone parent family, has young children or has a disabled parent. Therefore special attention needs to be paid to **the impact of recent, and any new, policy developments on households in which one worker is the maximum possible.**

It must always be recognised that work cannot be the answer for all parents. For example, for many parents with disabilities and/or with young children or other caring responsibilities, work is simply not an option. This emphasises the importance, once again, of ensuring that benefits are adequate to provide a decent standard of living for these families.

15.5 Movements between work and benefits

Persistent and severe childhood poverty appears particularly likely to occur around times of change in children's households, especially **movements between work and benefits**. The obvious way of ensuring that falls in income that precipitate children into persistent and severe poverty do not occur would be to **increase protection during times of transition between work and benefits.** This requires a three-fold strategy:

* first, to try and prevent transitions from work to benefits occurring by placing greater emphasis not just on getting parents into work (and, indeed, making work pay), but also on **ensuring that these jobs are retained**

* secondly, **ensuring that transitions from benefits to work are properly supported** so that a parent's taking a job does not precipitate their child(ren) into severe poverty

* thirdly, **ensuring that when transitions in the other direction, from work to benefits, do occur, families are protected from periods on extremely low incomes** – in other words, ensuring that benefits are received at these crucial times.

Policy has begun to move in the right direction in at least some of these areas, but is at different stages of development.

In Britain, policy concern with employment retention and progression is relatively recent, although an Employment Retention and Advancement project pilot scheme is due to commence in the Autumn of 2003. However, it must be said that evidence of the success of schemes to improve employment retention in other countries has, at best, been mixed (Kellard et al., 2002).

Policies aimed at assisting the transition from benefits to work (and ensuring that those in work are better supported) are more advanced. Working Tax Credit, the National Minimum Wage and, for children particularly, Child Tax Credit, which is paid irrespective of the work status of parents, may have 'smoothed' transitions from having no worker to one or more worker. Schemes such as the Job Grant (providing a one-off payment of £100 when moving into work for certain work-related items) and the Lone Parent Benefit Run-on (paying Housing Benefit and Council Tax Benefit for the first four weeks when an individual moves into work) have also been introduced. A number of further pilot initiatives have been signalled in the 2003 Budget, such as the worksearch premium for lone parents (£20 a week), continuing for the first year of work (at the higher level of £40 a week).

However, as these initiatives are heavily focused on the transition into work they will not assist those who make the transition from work to benefits – the third 'leg' of required policy outlined above – which, the evidence here has suggested, is also likely to be important in avoiding persistent and severe poverty for children. The only policy that the authors are aware of is the Rapid Reclaim system (which is an attempt to streamline the process of reclaiming benefits for people returning to them after full-time work of 12 weeks or less). However, a recent study found that just 3 per cent of benefit recipients were actually aware of this scheme (Woodland et al., 2003). Although the system should be applied regardless of recipients' knowledge of it, the study found that knowledge of such a scheme would be likely to encourage more recipients into work, as they were concerned (rightly it would appear from the results of this study) about their ability to move quickly back to benefits if their employment did not work out.

15.6 Lone parents and family transitions

Children in lone parent families were more likely to be poor than other children, using both measures of poverty. However, when other characteristics were controlled for, lone parenthood was no longer an important factor for severe poverty based on income and deprivation. So, in terms of providing necessities, it appears that the other characteristics associated with lone parenthood, such as no workers and receipt of benefits, were more important than lone parenthood *per se*. Using a low-income measure, a constant period of lone parenthood increased the chances of persistent poverty only (ie, without an experience of severe poverty), but it was **family transitions** (something that the PSE data could

not take into account) that were particularly associated with persistent and severe income poverty. Therefore, while a constant period of lone parenthood was associated with a long time in poverty, a movement to or from lone parenthood was more likely to be associated with a period of severe poverty in addition to persistent poverty. This highlights the importance of **ensuring families are aware of their benefit entitlements**, particularly when a change in their situation occurs.

It is to be anticipated that families experiencing such changes will not necessarily be able to, or wish to, start/return to work immediately after a relationship breakdown. Clearly, if children in these situations are to be protected from the extremes of poverty, particular measures need to be implemented to **ensure that families have an adequate income during this already stressful time**. Previous research with newly separated mothers highlighted that there was a minority who were not claiming benefits immediately after separation and that a number experienced delays in the processing of their claims (Leeming et al., 1994).

15.7 Family size and age of children

In both parts of the report, the greater the **number of children** in the household the more likely they were to experience poverty, but when other characteristics were controlled for this was no longer important for explaining income- and deprivation-based severe poverty. This means that other characteristics were more important than family size for explaining income- and deprivation-based poverty. For example, ethnicity may be such a factor – families of non-white ethnicity are known to have larger families, on average, than those of white ethnicity (see Section 15.8 for a discussion of the association between ethnicity and severe poverty). However, family size remained significant for experiences of short-term and persistent income poverty.

In both parts of the study, **younger children** in the household appeared to be associated with some degree of poverty. Policies have been introduced to assist families with the youngest children, such as disproportionate increases in the level of means-tested benefits paid for younger children, so that benefit rates for children of all ages have now been equalised. Additional help is also available for families with children in their first year of life through the Baby Addition in Child Tax Credit.

Although these initiatives are to be welcomed, it is worth noting that in the UK a larger amount of Child Benefit is paid for the oldest child in the family than for subsequent children. This is in contrast to some European countries, which pay more for second and subsequent children than for a first or only child (for example, Belgium). Whilst the proposed benefit levels for the new Child Tax Credit pay a similar amount for each child, because the Family Element is paid just once to all families with children, however many children there are in the family, and because Child Benefit will continue to be paid at a higher rate for oldest children, **larger families will continue to be relatively disadvantaged.**

15.8 Ethnicity

Children of **non-white ethnicity** were more likely to be in severe poverty when an income- and deprivation-based measure was used, even when other characteristics were taken into account. This was not the case when just an income-based measure was used – although non-white children were more likely to be in income poverty, this was not a significant factor when other characteristics were taken into account. Therefore it appears that non-white children, and their parents, were more likely to be deprived of necessities. One possible reason is that these families were less likely to have other sources of financial help available to them with which to purchase necessities when money was short. As evidence from the PSE on financial exclusion has revealed, minority ethnic families were much less likely than white families to, for example, have regular savings of at least £10 a week and to have a bank or building society account (Goodwin et al., 2002). In addition, in both surveys the sample sizes for children of non-white ethnicity were very small, so small that no distinction between different ethnicities could be made, differences which are vitally important to experiences of poverty (Department for Work and Pensions, 2003a). So to understand why it appears that minority ethnic children were more likely to lack necessities, and to identify any variation between different ethnicities, **a new large-scale quantitative survey to investigate the poverty situation of children in minority ethnic families** would be needed.

15.9 Education

In both parts of the report, parents not having any **educational qualifications** increased the chances of children being in severe (and non-severe) poverty, even when other characteristics were taken into account. Although there were reasonably large proportions of children in poverty whose parents did have (the highest level of) qualifications, it seems likely that **improving parents' attainment will improve children's chances of avoiding poverty**. Policies have been introduced, or announced, to do just that, such as the Employer Training Pilots (in which firms offer low-skilled workers paid time off to train). The government is also 'planning to publish a Skills Strategy in June 2003, setting a framework for action by government, individuals and employers to tackle deficiencies in the UK's skills base' (HM Treasury, 2003).

Analysis in Part 2 suggested that young people were well aware of the importance of education. Perhaps most importantly for policy, the fact that all young people were equally committed to doing well at school is highly encouraging. Yet smaller proportions of children in each poverty group intended to stay on after 16 years than was apparent among children who had not experienced poverty. Policies to **encourage young people from poorer backgrounds to remain in education**, such as Educational Maintenance Allowance and the Connexions Service, are likely to be of vital importance to their future, particularly given the association between lack of parental qualifications and poverty noted above.

15.10 Local area and housing

Clear links between poverty and exclusion experiences related to **local area and housing** were found in both parts of the report. Living in local authority housing was highly associated with all forms of poverty, even when all other characteristics were taken into account. In other words, regardless of their household's employment status, family type, benefit receipt and so on, children in poverty were still more likely to live in local authority housing. The income measures used in both parts of the report were before housing costs. Many households living in local authority accommodation would be eligible for help with their housing costs and, therefore, it may be that, if the research could have used an after housing costs measure, the association between poverty and living in local authority accommodation would have not have been as strong. However, as with Income Support and Jobseeker's Allowance, not all those who are entitled to Housing Benefit (or Council Tax Benefit) actually receive it. The most recent estimates suggests that between 10,000 and 100,000 families with children are not claiming the Housing Benefit to which they are entitled (Department for Work and Pensions, 2003c). Again, greater efforts must be made to **ensure that take-up rates are improved**.

It was also clear that problems with housing, such as shortage of space, damp walls or floors and lack of adequate heating, were much greater for children in poverty, severe or otherwise. Housing quality is clearly vital for a child's well-being and is the only environmentally based indicator of social exclusion specifically for children and young people in *Opportunity for All*. The indicator specifically is: 'a reduction in the proportion of children who live in a home that falls below the set standard of decency'. The definition of a decent home is a home that meets all of the following criteria:

- It is above the current statutory minimum standard for housing.
- It is in a reasonable state of repair.
- It has reasonably modern facilities and services.
- It provides a reasonable degree of thermal comfort.

The fact that both severely and non-severely poor children were at a particularly high risk of poor housing quality, compared to their non-poor counterparts, suggests that **this housing indicator should continue to be of high priority**.

The poor quality of the neighbourhoods in which severely poor children live suggests that the government is right to **emphasise policies that are aimed at specific localities**, for example Sure Start, Neighbourhood Renewal and the New Deal for Communities. Concentration on deprived neighbourhoods continues with the Social Exclusion Unit's new project investigating the 'Barriers to employment and enterprise in deprived areas' and Education and Health Action Zones, all of which should be of great advantage to severely poor children. However, it is worth noting that not all children in (severe) poverty will be reached by such methods. There are pockets of poverty in affluent areas, a detail which these surveys could not examine.

15.11 Geography

The increased risk of poverty within **the Midlands** using both income and deprivation measures and persistent income poverty measures – even when other characteristics were controlled for – is an unexpected finding and one that cannot be immediately explained. Although housing costs have not been taken into account in this analysis, it would be anticipated that doing so would increase the likelihood of poverty in the South (see further below), but cannot explain why children in the Midlands should be worse off than those in the North, for example. It could be that the types of jobs available in the Midlands were less secure and/or there were more low-skilled, low-paid, jobs in that region. However, this clearly **requires a more in-depth inquiry** to determine exactly what factors have led to such findings.

Children in the South of England were at an increased risk of severe poverty using the income and deprivation measure. This could be because the high housing costs in that region were affecting parents' ability to afford necessities for themselves and their children, an explanation unlikely to account for the greater likelihood of poverty in the Midlands.

15.12 Money, savings and debt

Investigations of the overlap between (severe) poverty and experiences of **savings and debt** also have important policy implications. Part 1 suggested that it is difficult for children's families to make regular savings when they are in poverty (indeed, even when they are not in poverty). Part 2 showed that, over time, parents **do** make savings when they can afford to do so. However, it is hardly surprising that the worse the poverty status of the children, the less likely their parents were to be able to save for the future, and this needs to be borne in mind when policies to encourage saving are being developed. For example, the Saving Gateway, which currently proposes to offer a government-matched contribution for small savings, will expect people to commit savings for five years in order to receive the government's contribution. The evidence in this report suggests that five years is far too long. The fact that parents do save when they can, and save quite large amounts, emphasises **the need for flexible savings plans** that families can pay into in 'good' years, and take holidays from payments in bad years without penalties. In fact, dis-saving during periods of poverty makes eminent sense, and it may be highly optimistic (or even inappropriate) to expect low-income families prone to spells of poverty, particularly those who are parents, to keep money to one side for five years in order to accrue maximum government contributions, rather than spending money on the immediate needs of their children.

There must be concern about the relatively large proportion of children living in families which were unable, or found it particularly difficult, to pay for their housing and/or basic utilities within the home. In terms of the debts parents had, Part 2 revealed that children in poverty were no more likely to have parents in debt than children not in poverty, confirming other research which has

highlighted the reluctance of low-income families to get into debt (Middleton, 2002). However, if they were in debt, the **type** of debts that parents in poverty had was very different from the debts of those not in poverty. Perhaps most importantly, the analysis revealed the high proportion of children in persistent poverty only whose parents had debts to the Social Fund. In November 2002, around a half of Income Support and Jobseeker's Allowance claimants who were having deductions made to their benefit were repaying Social Fund debts (Department for Work and Pensions 2002c and 2002d). This highlights the need for **an urgent review of the Social Fund**.

The analysis of the BHPS Youth Questionnaire allowed an investigation of young people's experiences of money according to their poverty status. The results here support other evidence suggesting that young people in poverty were less likely to receive pocket money or undertake paid work and that, when they did so, in the main, they were likely to receive lower amounts of pocket money and be paid lower wages (Shropshire and Middleton, 1999). Qualitative work with children has found that children's understanding of money and financial services is greatly affected by the methods of financial management and the financial services used by their parents (Loumidis and Middleton, 2000). Results in this study support findings of different parental use of financial services by poverty status. There is clearly a need to **ensure that all children are taught about managing finance and use of financial services**.

15.13 Emotional well-being

Poverty, particularly severe poverty and persistent poverty, appears to affect the **emotional well-being** of children and parents, and the relationships which children have with their parents. This must also have implications for children's longer-term prospects. Policies to **ensure that families do not suffer long periods of low income** will, at the very basic level, help to ensure that children in Britain are living in families that can provide them with the support and opportunities they require to be successful in the present and in the future. In addition, at least until poverty targets are achieved, young people clearly need access to counselling and emotional support. The most appropriate avenues for this may be the Children's Fund and Connexions Services, which apply to England, and equivalent agencies for Wales and Scotland. These need to ensure that their policies take account of the emotional and health needs, as well as the material needs, of children and young people experiencing poverty. Connexions Services' personal advisers must have adequate training, resources and other support services to deal with the more complex problems that some children may face.

15.14 Children's participation

The two parts of the report have given clear indications that children in poverty, particularly severe poverty, were restricted in their participation in activities and access to services from which other children were able to benefit.

Part 1 found that severely poor children were significantly more likely than non-severely poor and non-poor children to be excluded from social activities that parents believed to be essential for all children. The lower proportion of severely poor children with access to children's services such as nearby and safe play facilities and youth and after-school clubs – services which allow children the opportunity to meet and play in a secure environment – must also be of particular concern. Part 2 showed the lower proportion of severely poor children who had friends visit their homes. Given that access to leisure and social activities is a critical part of a child's quality of life, these differences need immediate attention.

15.15 Measuring child poverty

The two complementary parts of this report also have important implications for **measuring child poverty** and, therefore, could have relevance for the areas of further work the government has suggested in the preliminary conclusions to its consultation on child poverty measurement.

15.15.1 Deprivation-based measures of poverty over time

Part 2 of the report, of necessity, defined childhood poverty in relation to income thresholds. By itself, income definitions can give only partial policy guidance to those who seek to improve the circumstances of Britain's children because, as demonstrated in Part 1 of this report, low incomes do not necessarily equate to poverty (other resources can cover times of want). Similarly, higher incomes do not necessarily imply the absence of poverty. This seems particularly likely if, as a result of a recent poverty spell, resources have diminished to such an extent that an enduring spell of higher income is required to replenish resources. In essence, because arbitrary thresholds are used to measure income poverty, they do not and cannot reflect whether members of a family have an (in)adequate income to obtain all the necessities that they require. It is therefore highly desirable that longitudinal data resources become available in the future that allow for the construction of **deprivation-based measures of poverty over time**, so that persistent poverty can be measured using both income and deprivation measures. Such measures would be invaluable for identifying the circumstances under which income/other resources become inadequate to provide necessities and, in turn, when they become adequate to do so.

The Department for Work and Pension's Families and Children Study (FACS) – a partly longitudinal survey – appears to provide an opportunity to assess the government's achievements in reducing income poverty and deprivation. It currently includes a number of measures of deprivation, a few of which are similar to those in the PSE (see Vegeris and McKay, 2002, for details). There are a number of issues of concern regarding the specific items and activities included in the FACS lists that cannot be addressed here. However, the most important point for the measurement of child poverty is the fact that, while some of the indicators are specifically child-related, such as 'two pairs of weatherproof shoes for each child', others do not allow the experiences of children to be disaggregated from those of adults in the same household. This report has emphasised the importance of understanding the extent to which parents go without to protect their children from the effects of poverty and, therefore, the depth of poverty that must prevail before children are impacted upon, something that the indicators in FACS cannot currently assess.

15.15.2 Child-based indicators

The research has shown the enormous potential, and importance, of **including child-based indicators of poverty and social exclusion** when measuring child poverty and social exclusion. This may seem fairly obvious but, until recently, this has been lacking. The use of the child-based necessities measure in Part 1 clearly shows that letting poverty impact upon their children (in a material sense at least) is a last resort for parents. It also indicates what it is that children have to go without when parents are forced to let poverty impact upon their children.

Both the surveys analysed in this report have also shown the immense potential in developing **social exclusion measures specifically for children**. The Youth Questionnaire of the BHPS goes one stage further and asks young people themselves about their experiences. Analysis has revealed that young people appear to be very much affected, at least in some aspects of their lives, by their experiences of poverty, highlighting the importance of not just being concerned with child poverty because of the impacts it may have for children's future outcomes as adults (as much research does), but to be concerned because of **the impact poverty has on children's current lives** *as children*. In other words, we should be as concerned with children's 'well-being' as with their 'well-becoming'. This seems to be central to the approach of the Children and Young People's Unit which has said that 'At the heart of the Unit's approach is a recognition that we should have high expectations for every child and should work to ensure that provision for children and young people is designed to give everyone of them an equal opportunity to develop' (Children and Young People's Unit, 2001b, p.1). The efforts to measure the experiences of children and young people could be developed further, in the Youth Questionnaire or other surveys, to include questions like those in the PSE that have attempted to operationalise and measure social exclusion for children, and other questions such as their views regarding their housing, their local area and the services within it.

15.15.3 Childhood poverty and social exclusion – a multiple problem

Finally, it is important to emphasise that poverty has multiple manifestations and social exclusion is multi-dimensional. Therefore, a greater understanding of the different manifestations and dimensions, and their inter-relationships, is crucial to our understanding of child poverty. This means **ensuring that these different dimensions are measured in the same survey.** For example, the indicators in *Opportunity for All* are not measured in the same survey and therefore lack this understanding. Including different dimensions within one survey will make it easier to tailor policies that can genuinely improve the circumstances of British children and meet the ultimate goal of a country without child poverty.

Endnotes

Chapter 1

1 Equivalisation is the process by which household income is adapted to take into account the size of the household. For example, if a household with one adult and a household with two adults and two children both had weekly incomes of £200, it is clear that the £200 would go much further in the single person household than in the couple with children household. Therefore, equivalisation would reduce the income of the couple with children so that it was 'equivalent' to that of the single person household.

2 Unfortunately neither of the surveys used as data sources for this report included Northern Ireland so that the analysis is restricted to children in England, Scotland and Wales. In what follows, the combination of these three countries has been referred to as 'Britain', in line with the two surveys analysed. However, it is recognised that, strictly speaking, this should read Great Britain.

3 See, for example, Bradshaw, J. (ed.), 2001.

4 For a useful summary of these debates and definitions see Burchardt, T., Le Grand, J. and Piachaud, D., 2002.

5 However, there are also drawbacks to an after housing costs measure of income because it does not take into account the improved housing quality that higher housing costs may represent. See Hills, 2001.

6 For an analysis of poverty in London see Greater London Authority, 2002.

Chapter 2

1 See Annex C for a summary of how these measures are created.

Chapter 3

1 The original child deprivation measure included both items and activities. However, as lack of activities is perhaps more a reflection of social exclusion than poverty, it was decided that for the dimensions of poverty only the items should be retained in the list.

Remaining, therefore, were necessities in the following groups: food, clothing, educational development and environmental items. Using the original methodology to determine a cut-off point for deprivation (see Annex C) suggested that children could be defined as deprived if they lacked one or more of the items because they could not be afforded.

2 In addition, it is important to use such a measure as well as income because it may be that the household has high housing costs, the household may have debts that need to be repaid (both leaving a small disposable income) or income may have only recently increased, meaning that the household is still building up its assets. All possibilities could mean that necessities were lacked despite not being income poor.

As with the children's measure, the parent's deprivation measure included both items and activities and, for the same reasons, only the items were retained in the measure. Using the same methodology as for the children, the cut-off point for parent's deprivation was set at lacking two or more items because they could not be afforded.

3 This relationship between changes in income and deprivation of necessities is graphically presented in Gordon et al., 2000.

4 Income was equivalised using a scale developed for the PSE survey. See Gordon et al., 2000 for details.

5 The average incomes of these two groups of children were not significantly different from any of the other groups. This may be, in part, because there were too few cases for the significance test to find differences that did exist.

6 It is interesting to note that work using a number of adult measures of poverty has also found that the more dimensions of poverty on which adults are poor, the greater their differences from adults who are not poor (Bradshaw and Finch, forthcoming).

7 The combinations of permutations that make up the non-severely poor group should be borne in mind in what follows. These groups vary in a number of ways (such as average income, and the type and number of necessities lacking), variations that are masked when they are combined into a single group.

Chapter 4

1 This variable was created from information collected during the 1991 census. Areas were split into enumeration districts for the census enumerators. A count was then made of the usual resident population within the enumeration districts.

2 It should be noted that this analysis could only be undertaken for children who had data for each of the characteristics included in the analysis – a total of 714 cases. Some of the characteristics (eg, ethnicity, child's illness status) were collected in the General Household Survey to which the PSE was attached. Therefore, children born between the two surveys are particularly likely to be under-represented in this analysis.

3 This requires a 'reference child' as a basis for comparing these differences. The characteristics of the reference child were chosen as the category in each characteristic included in the analysis which had the lowest proportion of children in poverty. Therefore, the reference child for this analysis was:
- with at least one full-time worker or more than two workers in the household
- in an 'other' family type
- aged 11–16
- with two children in the family
- of white ethnicity
- living in owner-occupied accommodation
- with no ill parents
- not ill themselves
- not in receipt of IS/JSA
- with parent(s) educated to A level standard or higher
- living in an area of less than 1,000 residents
- living in Scotland
- with a youngest child aged 11–16.

Chapter 5

1 The original child necessities measure of deprivation (Gordon et al., 2000) included both items and activities. However, activities were excluded from the analysis of poverty reported in Chapters 3

and 4 since they seemed more appropriately considered in this study as a measure of social exclusion.

2 In all the investigations of mean social exclusion, a one-way anova test was performed on the difference between the mean scores. Significance was of at least 95 per cent.

3 For certain of the analyses that follow, small numbers of children mean that some of the results require a degree of caution in their acceptance. These are presented in parentheses in Table 5.3.

4 These differences were statistically significant at conventional levels.

5 The figures provided exclude those parents who reported that they did not know whether or not their child(ren) had been bullied (6 per cent) or accused of bullying (3 per cent).

6 The figures provided exclude those parents who reported that they did not know whether or not their child(ren) had been suspended from school (2 per cent).

Chapter 6

1 The reverse also seems to be true, ie, that mental health problems can lead to poverty.

Chapter 8

1 Net income provides a much more accurate estimation of resources available to the household than gross income and therefore, in almost all cases, poverty research uses net income. In addition, net income was used in Part 1 of this report and for consistency it was important that Part 2 should also use net income.

2 They have also created annual net income data (for details of these derived net incomes, see Bardasi et al., 1999, and Bardasi et al., 2001).

3 However, there remained important differences between the two net income measures in the two parts of the research. These are described in Annex E.

4 In fact the sample was a total of 2,870 children. However, net income data was available only for households in which all adults had answered questions regarding their income and, therefore, the final sample was reduced to this figure.

5 The BHPS 'longitudinal enumerated individual weight' for the last year that a child was present in the sample has been applied.

Chapter 9

1 Derived from National Statistics mid 1991–2001 population estimates of Great Britain, with an estimated 14,207,500 children aged 0–19.

2 Once the BHPS 'matures', so that data for the whole period of childhood is available, a more sophisticated, less arbitrary, categorisation will be possible.

3 It needs to be borne in mind that this analysis covers just five years of a child's life and we do not know what occurred in the child's life before and after these years. Analysts call this 'censoring' and, in this case, the analysis is both 'left-hand' and 'right-hand' censored because we do not know what occurred before (left-hand) and after (right-hand) the five years of analysis. This means that when this section reports a child being in severe poverty, for example, for the first time, it means the first time **in these five years**, and when it reports severe poverty lasted for one year, it means one year **in these five years**. It could be the case that the child had already been in and out of severe poverty before the start of the five-year period, or that the period of severe poverty continued well beyond the last year that the child was included in the analysis. Of course, in addition, as explained in the previous chapter, the analysis uses weekly income and therefore numerous additional changes between poverty states could have taken place in the other weeks of the year.

4 In other words, one which was observed to finish within the five year observation period, whether the start was observed or not.

5 These calculations are based on observed spell endings and would require more detailed and complex transition models to confirm the findings than was possible in this report.

6 In other words, there could have been a gradual deterioration in their income circumstances between the two time periods when measurement took place.

7 Indeed, the proportion of children experiencing severe poverty over the whole five years, rather than just at the week of interviews, is likely to have been higher.

Chapter 10

1 This analysis does not distinguish between full- and part-time workers. Although this would have been desirable, numbers in the sample were too small.

2 As noted, employment status refers to the week before interview. Therefore continuous work literally means that the household had worker(s) at every interview. It is possible that periods between interviews were spent without workers.

3 Other benefits were not analysed because small numbers of recipients would mean that the analysis would not be robust.

4 This question was asked in all waves with the exception of Wave 9, when instead the respondent was asked whether their health limited their daily activities a lot, a little or not at all. The respondent was defined as being ill if their daily activities were limited a little or a lot by their health.

5 Children in short-term and severe poverty have been excluded from this analysis because their small sample size resulted in the model producing unreliable estimates.

6 Such a technique requires a reference group from which all other characteristics are compared. In this case the reference group is a child who:
• lived in a household always with workers
• lived in a household that had always had the same number of workers or that had made a transition between two or more, one and no workers

- had no years in a lone parent family
- had no years in rented accommodation
- had no years with an ill adult
- had no transitions or one transition between ill and no ill adults in the household
- lived in a household which had five years with work as the main source of income
- had no years in receipt of benefit
- had no transition or one transition between receipt of benefit and no receipt of benefit
- lived in the north of England for the majority of years
- lived in a one-child family on average
- had the same number of children in all years
- was aged 15–19
- had a youngest child in the household aged 15–19 on average
- had parents with no education qualifications
- lived in an all-white household.

7 Work refers to economic activity in the week before the interview. It is possible that someone in the household actually worked at some point during the intervals between at least one of a pair of successive interviews.

8 Technically, these 'chances' refer to odds ratios, which are multiplicative.

9 It should be also be recalled that employment status is measured in the BHPS in the week prior to the interview, whereas income is calculated between September and August of the whole year prior to the interview.

Chapter 12

1 For all children significant (p<0.05) differences between:
- persistent and severe poverty and no poverty
- persistent poverty only and no poverty, and short-term poverty only
- short-term poverty only and no poverty.

For children whose parents saved significant (p<0.05) differences between:
- persistent and severe poverty and no poverty

- persistent poverty only and no poverty
- short-term poverty only and no poverty.

2 But not significantly greater than other children experiencing poverty.

3 For all children significant differences (p<0.05) between:
- persistent and severe poverty and no poverty
- persistent poverty only and no poverty.

For children whose parents had debts, significant differences (p<0.05) between:
- persistent and severe poverty and no poverty
- persistent poverty only and no poverty
- persistent poverty only and short-term poverty only.

4 Persistent and severe poverty and persistent poverty only both significantly (p<0.05) greater than no poverty and short-term poverty only.

Chapter 13

1 These analyses exclude young people who did not have a mother or father, as appropriate.

2 'Professional/managerial' combines managers and administrators and professional occupations. 'Skilled occupation' combines associate professionals and technical occupations, clerical and secretarial occupations and craft and related occupations. 'Unskilled manual' combines personal and protective service occupations, sales occupations and plant and machine operatives. 'Other' is simply other occupations.

Chapter 15

1 The government does also include measures of health, education, housing and employment among its indicators of progress for tackling child poverty in *Opportunity for All.*

2 It has been suggested that deprivation indicators could become part of the Family Resources Survey (Department for Work and Pensions, 2002b and 2003b).

3 The most recent estimates, for 2000/01, found that up to 11 per cent of couples with children and 7 per cent of lone parents were not taking up the Income Support to which they were entitled (Department for Work and Pensions, 2003c). For Jobseeker's Allowance, among couples with children, non take-up was estimated to be between 11 and 21 per cent (ibid.). Working Families Tax Credit (the predecessor to the Child Tax Credit and Working Tax Credit) had much higher rates of non take-up. For 2000/01, the estimated non take-up rate for all families was between 35 and 38 per cent (Inland Revenue, 2002).

4 The latest figures, for November 2002, show that 31 per cent of Income Support claimants and 27 per cent of Jobseeker's Allowance claimants were having deductions made, with average deductions of £10.44 and £8.28 respectively (Department for Work and Pensions, 2002c and 2002d).

References

Adelman, L., Middleton, S. and Ashworth, K. (2003) *Dimensions of Poverty and Social Exclusion in Childhood: An analysis of the Poverty and Social Exclusion Survey of Britain.* CRSP Working Paper No. 463. Loughborough University: Centre for Research in Social Policy.

Adelman, L., Middleton, S. and Ashworth, K. (2002) *Child Poverty and Social Exclusion.* PSE Working Paper No. 19.

Ashworth, K., Walker, R., Middleton, S., Kellard, K., Peaker, A. and Thomas, M. (1994) "Keeping Up Appearances': Peer Pressure and Children's Clothes' in Middleton, S., Ashworth, K. and Walker, R. (eds.) *Family Fortunes: Pressures on parents and children in the 1990s.* London: Child Poverty Action Group.

Bardasi, E., Jenkins, S. and Rigg, J. (1999) *Documentation for Derived Current and Annual Net Household Income Variables, BHPS Waves 1–7.* Working Paper 99-25, Institute for Social and Economic Research, University of Essex.

Bardasi, E., Jenkins, S. and Rigg, J. (2001) *Derived Current and Annual Net Household Income Variables to Accompany BHPS Waves 1–9.* Institute for Social and Economic Research, University of Essex.

Bradbury, B., Jenkins, S. and Micklewright, J. (eds.) (2001) *The Dynamics of Child Poverty in Industrialised Countries.* Cambridge: Cambridge University Press.

Bradshaw, J. and Finch, N. (forthcoming) 'Overlaps in Dimensions of Poverty' *Journal of Social Policy.*

Bradshaw, J. (ed.) (2001) *Poverty: The outcomes for children.* London: Family Policy Studies Centre/National Children's Bureau.

Burchardt, T., Le Grand, J. and Piachaud, D. (2002) 'Introduction' in Hills, J., Le Grand, J. and Piachaud, D. (eds.) *Understanding Social Exclusion.* Oxford: Oxford University Press.

Children and Young People's Unit (2001a) *Learning to Listen: Core principles for the involvement of children and young people.* London: Children and Young People's Unit.

Children and Young People's Unit (2001b) *Tomorrow's Future: Building a strategy for children and young people.* London: Children and Young People's Unit.

Department for Culture, Media and Sport (1999) *Arts and Sport.* London: Department for Culture, Media and Sport.

Department for Work and Pensions (2001) *Opportunity for All: Making progress.* Cm 5260, London: The Stationery Office.

Department for Work and Pension (2002a) *Opportunity for All: Fourth annual report 2002.* Cm 5598, London: The Stationery Office.

Department for Work and Pensions (2002b) *Measuring Child Poverty. A consultation document.* London: Department for Work and Pensions.

Department for Work and Pensions (2002c) *Income Support Quarterly Statistical Enquiry November 2002.* London: Department for Work and Pensions.

Department for Work and Pensions (2002d) *Jobseeker's Allowance Quarterly Statistical Enquiry November 2002.* London: Department for Work and Pensions.

Department for Work and Pensions (2003a) *Households Below Average Income 1994/5 – 2001/02.* Corporate Document Services.

Department for Work and Pensions (2003b) *Measuring Child Poverty Consultation: Preliminary conclusions.* London: Department for Work and Pensions.

Department for Work and Pensions (2003c) *Income Related Benefits Estimates of Take-up in 2000/2001.* London: National Statistics.

Department of Health (1999) *Improving Shopping Access for People Living in Deprived Neighbourhoods.* London: Department of Health.

Department of Social Security (1999) *Opportunity for All: Tackling poverty and social exclusion – first annual report.* Cm 4455, London: The Stationery Office.

Department of Social Security (2000) *Opportunity for All, One Year On: Making a difference.* Cm 4865, London: The Stationery Office.

Egerton, M. (2002) 'Family transmission of social capital: Differences by social class, education and public sector employment', *Sociological Research Online*, Volume 7, Issue 3, http://www.socresonline.org.uk/7/3/egerton.html.

Ermisch, J., Francesconi, M. and Pevalin, D. J. (2001) *Outcomes of Poverty for Children.* Department for Work and Pensions Research Report No. 158. Leeds: Corporate Document Services.

Goodwin, D., Adelman, L. and Middleton, S. (2002) *Debt, Money Management and Access to Financial Services.* PSE Working Paper No. 8. Bristol: Townsend Centre for International Poverty Research, University of Bristol.

Gordon, D. and Pantazis, C. (eds.) (1997) *Breadline Britain in the 1990s.* Aldershot: Ashgate.

Gordon, D., Adelman, L., Ashworth, K., Bradshaw, J., Levitas, R., Middleton, S., Pantazis, C., Patsios, D., Payne, S., Townsend, P. and Williams, J. (2000) *Poverty and Social Exclusion in Britain.* York: Joseph Rowntree Foundation.

Greater London Authority (2002) *London Divided: Income inequality and poverty in the capital.* London: Greater London Authority.

Hill, M. and Jenkins, S. (2001) 'Poverty among British children: chronic or transitory?' in Bradbury, B., Jenkins, S. and Micklewright, J. (eds.) *The Dynamics of Child Poverty in Industrialised Countries.* Cambridge: Cambridge University Press.

Hills, J. (2001) 'Measurement of income poverty and deprivation: The British approach' in *Indicators of Progress. A discussion of approaches to monitor the government's strategy to tackle poverty and social exclusion.* CASE report 13. London: Centre for Analysis of Social Exclusion.

HM Treasury (1999a) *Initiatives to Tackle Financial Exclusion.* London: HM Treasury.

HM Treasury (1999b) *Access to Financial Services.* London: HM Treasury.

HM Treasury (2003) *Budget 2003: Building a Britain of economic strength and social justice.* London: HM Treasury.

Inland Revenue (2002) *Working Families' Tax Credit Estimates of Take-up Rates in 2000–01.* London: Inland Revenue.

Kellard, K., Adelman, L., Cebulla, A. and Heaver C. (2002) *From Job Seekers to Job Keepers: Job retention, advancement, and the role of in-work support programmes.* DWP Research Report 170. Leeds: Corporate Document Services.

Layte, R., Nolan, B. and Whelan, C. (2000) 'Targeting Poverty: Lessons from Ireland's National Anti-Poverty Strategy' *Journal of Social Policy*, 29 (4) pp. 553–75.

Leeming, A., Unell, J. and Walker, R. (1994) *Lone Mothers.* DSS Research Report No. 30 London: Corporate Document Services.

Loumidis, J. and Middleton, S. (2000) *A Cycle of Disadvantage? Financial exclusion in childhood.* London: Financial Services Authority.

Mack, J. and Lansley, S. (1985) *Poor Britain.* London: George Allen.

Marsh, A. and Perry, J. (2003) *Family change 1999 to 2001.* DWP Research Report 180. Leeds: Corporate Document Services.

Micklewright, J. (2002) *Social Exclusion and Children: A European view for a US Debate.* Innocenti Working Paper No. 90, Florence: UNICEF Innocenti Research Centre.

Middleton, S. (2002) 'Coping for the children: Low income families and financial management' in *How People on Low Incomes Manage their Finances.* Economic and Social Research Council.

Middleton, S. and Adelman, L. (2003) 'The Poverty and Social Exclusion Survey of Britain: Implications for the assessment of social security provision for children in Europe' in Bradshaw, J. (ed.) *Children and Social Security.* International Studies in Social Security Volume 8. Aldershot: Ashgate Publishing Ltd.

Middleton, S., Ashworth, K. and Walker, R. (1994) *Family Fortunes: Pressures on parents and children in the 1990s.* London: Child Poverty Action Group.

Middleton, S. and Loumidis, J. (2001) 'Young people, poverty and part-time work' in Mizen, P., Pole, C. and Bolton, A. (eds) *Hidden Hands: International perspectives on children's work and labour.* London: Routledge Falmer, pp. 24–36.

Payne, S. (2000) *Poverty, Social Exclusion and Mental Health: Findings from the 1999 PSE survey.* PSE Working Paper No. 15.

Ridge, T. (2002) *Childhood Poverty and Social Exclusion: From a child's perspective.* Bristol: The Policy Press.

Shropshire, S. and Middleton, S. (1999) *Small Expectations: Learning to be poor?* York: Joseph Rowntree Foundation.

Social Exclusion Unit (1999) *Schools Plus: Building learning communities.* London: Department for Education and Skills.

Social Exclusion Unit (2001) *Preventing Social Exclusion: Report by the Social Exclusion Unit.* London: The Cabinet Office.

Social Exclusion Unit (2002) *Making the Connections: Transport and social exclusion interim findings.* London: The Cabinet Office.

Social Protection Committee (2001) *Report on indicators in the field of poverty and social exclusion.* See http://register.consilium. eu.int/pdf/en/01/st13/13509en1.pdf.

Stone, W. and Hughes, J. (2001) *Social Capital: Linking family and community?* Paper presented at Family Strengths Conference, 2–5 December 2001, Newcastle, Australia.

Sutherland, H. (2001) *Five Labour Budgets (1997–2001): Impacts on the distribution of household incomes and on child poverty.* Microsimulation Unit Research Note no. 41, May 2001.

Townsend, P. (1979) *Poverty in the United Kingdom.* London: Allen Lane and Penguin Books.

United Nations Development Programme (1993) *Human Development Report 1993: People's participation.* Oxford: Oxford University Press (or http://hdr.undp.org/reports/global/1993/en/).

Vegeris, S. and McKay, S. (2002) *Low/Moderate-Income Families in Britain: Changes in living standards.* DWP Research Report 164. Leeds: Corporate Document Services.

Weich, S. and Lewis, G. (1998) 'Poverty, unemployment and common mental disorders: population based cohort study' *British Medical Journal* Vol 317, pp. 115–19.

Woodland, S., Mandy, W. and Miller, M. (2003) *Easing the Transition into Work (Part 2 – client survey).* DWP Research Report 186. Leeds: Corporate Document Services.

Annex A
Items and activities regarded as necessary

Table A 1 Percentage of parents regarding items and activities as necessary

	Percentage of parents regarding item as 'necessary'
New, properly fitted shoes	96
Bed and bedding for self	96
Warm, waterproof coat	95
Fresh fruit or vegetables at least one a day	93
Celebrations on special occasions	92
Three meals a day	91
Books of own	90
Play group at least once a week (pre-school age children)*	89
Hobby/leisure activity*	88
All required school uniform*	88
Toys (eg, dolls, play figures)*	85
Educational games	84
At least seven pairs of new underpants	84
Meat/fish/vegetarian equivalent twice a day	76
Bedrooms for every child of different sex over 10 years*	76
Carpet in bedroom	75
At least four pairs of trousers	74
School trip at least once a term*	73
Swimming at least once a month	71
At least four jumpers/cardigans/sweatshirts	71
Garden in which to play	68
Some new, not 2nd hand, clothes	67
Construction toys	66
Holiday away from home at least one week a year	63
Bike: new/second-hand*	60
Leisure equipment*	57
Friends round for tea/snack fortnightly*	53

Key: * = age-related items

Italics = social activity

Annex B
Characteristics of children in severe poverty

Table B I Characteristics of children in severe poverty

Row per cent

	No poverty	Non-severe poverty	Severe poverty
Employment status***			
Two full-time workers	73	(26)	(1)
One full-time, one part-time worker	72	28	(<0.5)
One full-time worker	61	37	(2)
One or more part-time workers	22	70	(8)
More than two workers	(84)	(16)	0
No workers	(6)	56	38
Family type***			
Couple	63	34	3
Lone parent	21	54	25
Other	64	33	(4)
Income quintile***			
Five	94	(7)	0
Four	79	(21)	0
Three	68	32	0
Two	53	47	0
One	(10)	59	31
Age of child***			
0–1 year	48	48	(4)
2–4 years	59	32	9
5–10 years	51	41	8
11–16 years	60	33	8
Age of youngest child in household**			
0–1 year	46	49	(6)
2–4 years	59	32	9
5–10 years	52	41	7
11–16 years	67	26	(7)
Number of children***			
1	53	38	9
2	63	33	5
3	40	52	8
4 or more	(54)	29	17
Ethnic group***			
White	58	36	6
Non-white	(34)	44	22

continued opposite

Table B 1 Characteristics of children in severe poverty *continued*

Row per cent

	No poverty	Non-severe poverty	Severe poverty
Tenure***			
Own	69	29	2
Rent local authority	(9)	69	21
Rent other	31	48	21
One or more parent has long-standing illness			
No	57	36	7
Yes	47	44	9
Child has long-standing illness			
No	55	37	9
Yes	56	39	(5)
Household receiving IS/JSA***			
No	65	34	(1)
Yes	(8)	56	36
Highest education level of parent(s)***			
A levels or higher	71	26	3
GCE or equivalent	47	44	9
CSE or equivalent	(18)	79	(4)
None	(22)	55	23
Population size**			
1 million or more	49	39	12
100,000 to 999,999	52	42	7
10,000 to 99,999	51	43	(6)
1,000 to 9,999	66	26	(8)
Less than 1,000	70	25	(5)
Government office region – grouped			
North	57	36	(7)
Midlands	57	33	10
South	52	41	7
Wales	(49)	47	(4)
Scotland	64	25	(12)
All children	55	37	8

Unweighted base = 729–769 children (variation due to missing values)

Significance * p<0.05; ** p<0.01; *** p<0.001

Annex C
Creation of the child and adult deprivation measures

C1 Introduction

The method by which the adult deprivation index and child deprivation index were constructed is described in detail in Appendix 2 and Appendix 3 of the main PSE report, respectively (Gordon et al., 2000). These two procedures varied slightly. In this study, the procedure used to create the child deprivation index in the original PSE study was followed to recreate new poverty measures for both adults and children. This procedure, which contains three main elements, – testing validity, testing reliability and identifying a poverty threshold – is described in summary in this annex. Readers interested in a more detailed explanation should refer to the main PSE report.

The original child and adult deprivation measures included as necessities both material items and social activities. However, as we wished to investigate access to activities as part of our investigation of social exclusion, only **items** were retained in the indices.

Child items that over half of parents believed to be necessary were retained for consideration in the child index, and adult items that over half of adults believed to be necessary were retained for consideration in the adult index. This resulted in 20 of the 23 child items being retained and 26 of the 39 adult items being retained.

C2 Validating the items

Items with no significant association with four other measures of poverty were excluded from further analysis, as it would suggest that they were not valid indicators of deprivation. For the child items, only two items (toys and own books) were found to be independent of one of the other poverty measures used to test the association. However, these two items showed a positive association with the remaining three out of the four subjective measures, and so were accepted as valid indicators of deprivation. Thus, as all necessary child items were retained in the analysis, all necessary adult items were also retained in the analysis, although there was evidence in the original analysis that there may have been a limited number of items whose validity could be contested.

C3 The reliability of the scale

All items were next assessed to establish if they were measuring the same single underlying dimension of deprivation. In other words, were they all measuring the same type of deprivation or were they measuring different types of deprivation? For example, it may have been the case that there was a clothing type of deprivation (including the clothing items) which was distinct from a food type of deprivation (including the food items) and so on.

Reliability can be measured in a number of ways. For this analysis a statistical method called Cronbach's alpha was used. This analysis highlights which items should be excluded if the reliability of the scale is to be improved. The exclusion of two child items (separate bedrooms for opposite sex siblings aged over 10 years and a garden in which to play) would have improved the child index by a small extent. However, as the gain was minimal, and there is no established way to test the significance of the improvement, it was decided to retain all items in the index. Similarly, exclusion of five of the adult items would have slightly improved the reliability of the scale. However, as with the children's index, the gain was minimal (gains in the region of 0.001).

C4 Identifying a deprivation threshold

Finally, an exploration was undertaken to establish the appropriate threshold number of items of which a child/adult had to go without in order to classify the child/adult as deprived. Answering the question of how many items a child should be lacking before being considered deprived is not straightforward. The essential concept underlying the scale is that children lack necessities because their parents cannot afford to buy them (or adults lack necessities because they cannot afford to buy them). From this perspective, it is arguable that the current income should be reflected in the deprivation scores. However, there are many reasons why the two may not match. For example, a family whose income has recently dropped may be protected against deprivation by drawing on savings or because a number of the necessities are linked to a life span that may outlast short periods of deprivation (eg, clothes and material goods).

A sequential approach was adopted whereby children first were classified as deprived if they lacked one or more necessities and not deprived otherwise. This was then extended to two or more items as deprived, and so forth. The extent to which deprived children were more similar to each other, while at the same time non-deprived children were more similar to each other – so that differences between the two groups were maximised – was established using discriminant function analysis (DFA).

DFA predicts group membership (deprived versus non-deprived) according to a set of explanatory variables indexing children's characteristics. Income is the main criterion by which the two groups were separated. However, controls were also required for family composition.

The results of the analysis suggested that the appropriate distinction for children was between no necessities and one or more necessities: the eigenvalue (that is, the value that enables us to assess the extent of the difference between 'deprived' and 'non-deprived' children) was greatest for this distinction.

For adults the same method was applied. In this case the eigenvalue was greatest when a distinction of none and one versus two or more necessities was used. In other words, when parents lacked two or more necessities they could be classified as deprived.

C5 Summary

A scale measuring childhood deprivation was produced using 20 necessary items and for adult deprivation using 26 necessary items. The validity of the items was established because, generally, each adult and child item was significantly associated with other measures of poverty. In general, the child and adult items formed internally consistent measures of deprivation. Using the DFA results suggested a cut-off of one or more necessary items as the classification for deprivation for children, and of two or more necessary items for adults.

Annex D
Significant characteristics explaining non-severe and severe poverty

Table D 1 Significant characteristics explaining non-severe and severe poverty

	Compared to a non-poor child:	
	Odds of being non-severely poor if in a household with	**Odds of being severely poor if in a household with**
Part-time workers	6.00	
No workers	11.96	69.12
Non-white ethnicity		4.68
Local authority accommodation	7.96	7.27
In receipt of IS/JSA		9.40
South	2.70	4.02
Midlands		9.78
Parent has no educational qualifications	3.34	5.04
Youngest child aged 0–1 year	7.74	
Youngest child aged 5–10 years	3.15	

Unweighted base = 714 children

Note: All odds have a significance of at least 95 per cent.

Annex E
Differences between PSE and BHPS net income

- **Local taxes**. In the BHPS, local taxes are deducted from a household's net income. This deduction was not made in the PSE income measure.
- **Self-employment earnings**. In the BHPS, self-employment earnings refer to the most recent period for which a respondent kept accounts or has a record of gross earnings. These can be up to four years out of date. Therefore, these incomes have been up-rated in line with inflation. In the PSE income measure, respondents were asked what their self-employment earnings were in the past tax year.
- **Household net labour income**. In the BHPS, income tax, National Insurance contributions and occupational pension contributions were estimated and deducted from gross earnings. In the PSE income measure, employees were asked to give their net earnings and self-employed people were asked what their National Insurance contributions had been in the past tax year.

In addition, it should be noted that the median income of our BHPS child sample was lower than that of the PSE child sample. Households in which not all adult members had completed questionnaires did not have a net income created for the BHPS and therefore the lower median income could have arisen if, on average, these partial respondent households had a lower income than complete respondent households. However, other possible reasons might also explain this discrepancy.

Annex F
Sample used in Part 2 of this study

F1 Constructing the sample

In constructing the phases of childhood, it was important to ensure that each phase was of equal length so that poverty persistence would be measured over an equal number of years for each age group. For example, if we had one phase of children aged 0–4 years and another of children aged 5–11 years, the analysis would be measuring poverty persistence for the first phase over five years and the second phase over seven years.

Figure F 1 demonstrates how these 'cohorts' were established and helps to visualise how they work in practice. For example, in Cohort 1, a child who was aged less than 1 year in 1991 was followed

Figure F 1 Child cohorts

	Age	Wave 1 1991	Wave 2 1992	Wave 3 1993	Wave 4 1994	Wave 5 1995	Wave 6 1996	Wave 7 1997	Wave 8 1998	Wave 9 1999
Cohort 1	0	X	X	X	X	X				
	1		X	X	X	X	X			
	2			X	X	X	X	X		
	3				X	X	X	X	X	
	4					X	X	X	X	X
Cohort 2	5	X	X	X	X	X				
	6		X	X	X	X	X			
	7			X	X	X	X	X		
	8				X	X	X	X	X	
	9					X	X	X	X	X
Cohort 3	10	X	X	X	X	X				
	11		X	X	X	X	X			
	12			X	X	X	X	X		
	13				X	X	X	X	X	
	14					X	X	X	X	X
Cohort 4	15	X	X	X	X	X				
	16		X	X	X	X	X			
	17			X	X	X	X	X		
	18				X	X	X	X	X	
	19					X	X	X	X	X

until 1995 when he or she was 4 years old; a child who was aged less than 1 year in 1992 was followed until 1996 when he or she was 4 years old, and so on. For Cohort 2, children started in the analysis in the year in which they were 5 years old, for Cohort 3 when they were 10 years old and for Cohort 4 when they were 15 years old.

F2 Consequences for understanding recent policy

The majority of observations in this analysis relate to periods before the change of government in 1997 and subsequent policy initiatives aimed at remedying childhood poverty. This is inevitable given the current state of maturity of the BHPS. However, the findings should provide some useful indications as to whether policy interventions since 1997 are likely to improve the circumstances of children who are worst off, that is, those who are persistently and severely poor, and indications of further policy change that might be necessary.

In theory, it is also the case that the way in which the cohorts have been constructed could mean that children in our sample might have experienced different policy regimes. For example, children who were born in 1992 could have had different policy 'experiences' from those who were born in 1995. However, given that there was the same political party in government until 1997 and, given that new policies introduced post-election were unlikely to have had much effect by 1999, the last year of our sample, it seems safe to combine the cohorts in this way. As the BHPS matures it will be possible to comment on the impact of post-1997 policy interventions on children's lives.

Annex G
Absolute and equivalised levels of Income Support

Table G 1 Weekly Income Support levels in 1999 and 2002

	Weekly Income Support levels (£) (April 1999)	Weekly Income Support levels (£) (October 2002)
Lone Parent (aged 18 or over)	51.40	53.95
Couple (one or both aged 18 or over)	80.65	84.65
Dependent child aged under 11	20.20	33.50
Dependent child aged 11–16	25.90	33.50
Family Premium – couple	13.90	14.75
Family premium – lone parent	15.75	14.75

Table G 2 Equivalised Income Support levels for eight different family types, 1999

Family types	Income Support levels (£)	PSE equivalence scale	Equivalised Income Support levels (£)
Lone parent with one child under 11	87.35	1.15	75.96
Lone parent with one child 11–16	93.05	1.15	80.91
Lone parent with one child under 11 and one 11–16	113.25	1.45	78.10
Lone parent with three children, two under 11 and one 11–16	133.45	1.75	76.26
Couple with one child under 11	114.75	1.35	85.00
Couple with one child 11–16	120.45	1.35	89.22
Couple with one child under 11 and one 11–16	140.65	1.65	85.24
Couple with three children, two under 11 and one 11–16	160.85	1.95	82.49

Table G 3 Equivalised Income Support levels for eight different family types, 2003

Family types	Income Support levels (£)	PSE equivalence scale	Equivalised Income Support levels (£)
Lone parent with one child under 11	102.2	1.15	88.87
Lone parent with one child 11–16	102.2	1.15	88.87
Lone parent with one child under 11 and one 11–16	135.7	1.45	93.59
Lone parent with three children, two under 11 and one 11–16	169.2	1.75	96.69
Couple with one child under 11	132.9	1.35	98.44
Couple with one child 11–16	132.9	1.35	98.44
Couple with one child under 11 and one 11–16	166.4	1.65	100.85
Couple with three children, two under 11 and one 11–16	199.9	1.95	102.51

Annex H
Comparison between children in income and deprivation poverty and those in income only poverty

The first row of Table H 1 shows that the large majority of children who were in no poverty using the income and deprivation measure were also in no poverty using the income only definition – 93 per cent – and that the remainder were in non-severe poverty – 7 per cent. No children that were not in poverty using the income and deprivation measure were in severe poverty using the income only definition. The second row shows that children who were in non-severe poverty using the income and deprivation measure were most likely to change poverty groups when the income only definition was applied, with 50 per cent not in poverty using an income only definition, 38 per cent in non-severe poverty and 13 per cent now in

severe poverty. Of children who were in severe poverty using the income and deprivation measure of poverty, no children were not in poverty using the income only definition, 50 per cent were in non-severe poverty and a further 50 per cent of children were also in severe poverty using an income only definition (this is because the income only measure uses 'median' income and so, by definition, would only include 50 per cent of these children).

Despite these differences, with only an income poverty measure available, using the median incomes of the income and deprivation poverty groups seemed the most sensible compromise.

Table H 1 Comparison between children in income and deprivation poverty and those in income only poverty

Row per cent

PSE definition (income and deprivation)	Income definition (income only)		
	No poverty	Non-severe poverty	Severe poverty
No poverty	93	7	0
Non-severe poverty	50	38	13
Severe poverty	0	50	50

Annex I
Poverty persistence permutations

Table 11 Poverty persistence permutations

Number of years in:			Percentage of children	
no poverty	non-severe poverty	severe poverty		
No poverty:				**49.5**
5	0	0	49.5	
Short-term poverty only:				**17.8**
4	1	0	11.3	
3	2	0	6.5	
Short-term and severe poverty:				**3.8**
4	0	1	1.8	
3	1	1	1.6	
3	0	2	(0.4)	
Persistent poverty only:				**20.0**
2	3	0	7.1	
1	4	0	4.9	
0	5	0	8.0	
Persistent and severe poverty:				**8.8**
2	2	1	1.6	
2	1	2	(0.2)	
2	0	3	(0.2)	
1	3	1	2.4	
1	2	2	(0.4)	
1	1	3	(0.1)	
1	0	4	(0.1)	
0	4	1	2.4	
0	3	2	(0.9)	
0	2	3	(0.3)	
0	1	4	(0.1)	
0	0	5	(0.1)	

Annex J
Significant characteristics explaining poverty persistence and severity

Table J 1 Significant characteristics explaining poverty persistence and severity

	Short-term poverty only	Persistent poverty only	Persistent and severe poverty
Number of years without workers			
5			16.668
2	5.488		
1	4.749	3.665	4.494
Employment transitions			
2 or more and 1 worker	2.110		
Number of years in lone parent family			
5			0.398
3–4	4.627		
Number of years in rented accommodation			
5	2.765	4.567	2.738
Number of years with ill adult(s) in household			
3–4	2.829	4.083	5.926
1–2	1.737	2.357	
Transitions between ill and no ill adult			
2+ transitions		2.127	
Number of years work main source of income			
0		24.800	
1		44.583	
Main source of income transitions			
2+ transitions			24.388

continued overleaf

Table J 1 Significant characteristics explaining poverty persistence and severity *continued*

	Short-term poverty only	Persistent poverty only	Persistent and severe poverty
Number of years in receipt of benefits			
5	5.934		6.976
4	3.932	5.767	13.693
3	3.856	4.935	12.089
2			3.197
1	1.731		
Region lived in most years			
Midlands	1.739	3.274	3.627
Average number of children in household			
3 or more	4.180	4.820	11.626
2	2.013		2.525
Age of child			
5–9	2.406		
Highest parental educational qualifications			
Degree or higher	0.244	0.060	0.215
A level or equivalent	0.470	0.378	
Average age of youngest child in household			
0–4 years		10.914	9.741
5–9 years		4.443	
10–14 years		4.397	

Unweighted base = 1659 children

Note: All odds have a significance of at least 95 per cent.

Annex K
Necessity questions in the BHPS and PSE compared

Table K 1 shows the necessities that were included in the BHPS and the corresponding question in the PSE. It also presents the proportion of adults or parents who regarded these items as a necessity in the PSE and the proportions of adults and/or children going without the item because it could not be afforded in this survey.

Table K 1 Necessity questions in the BHPS and PSE compared

BHPS question	PSE question	Per cent necessary in PSE	Per cent cannot afford in PSE
Keep home adequately warm	Heating to warm living areas of the home	94 (adults)	1 (adults)
A week's annual holiday away from home	Holiday away from home once a year not with relatives (adult)	55 (adults)	18 (adults)
	Holiday away from home at least one week a year (child)	63 (parents)	22 (children)
Replace worn out furniture	Replace worn out furniture	54 (adults)	12 (adults)
Buy new, rather than 2nd hand, clothes	Buy new, rather than 2nd hand, clothes	48 (adults) 67 (parents)	5 (adults) 3 (children)
Eat meat, chicken, fish every second day	Meat, fish, or vegetarian equivalent every other day (adult)	79 (adults)	3 (adults)
	Meat, fish, or vegetarian equivalent twice a day (child)	76 (parents)	4 (children)
Have friends/family round for drink/meal once a month	Have friends/family round for drink/meal	64 (adults)	6 (adults)